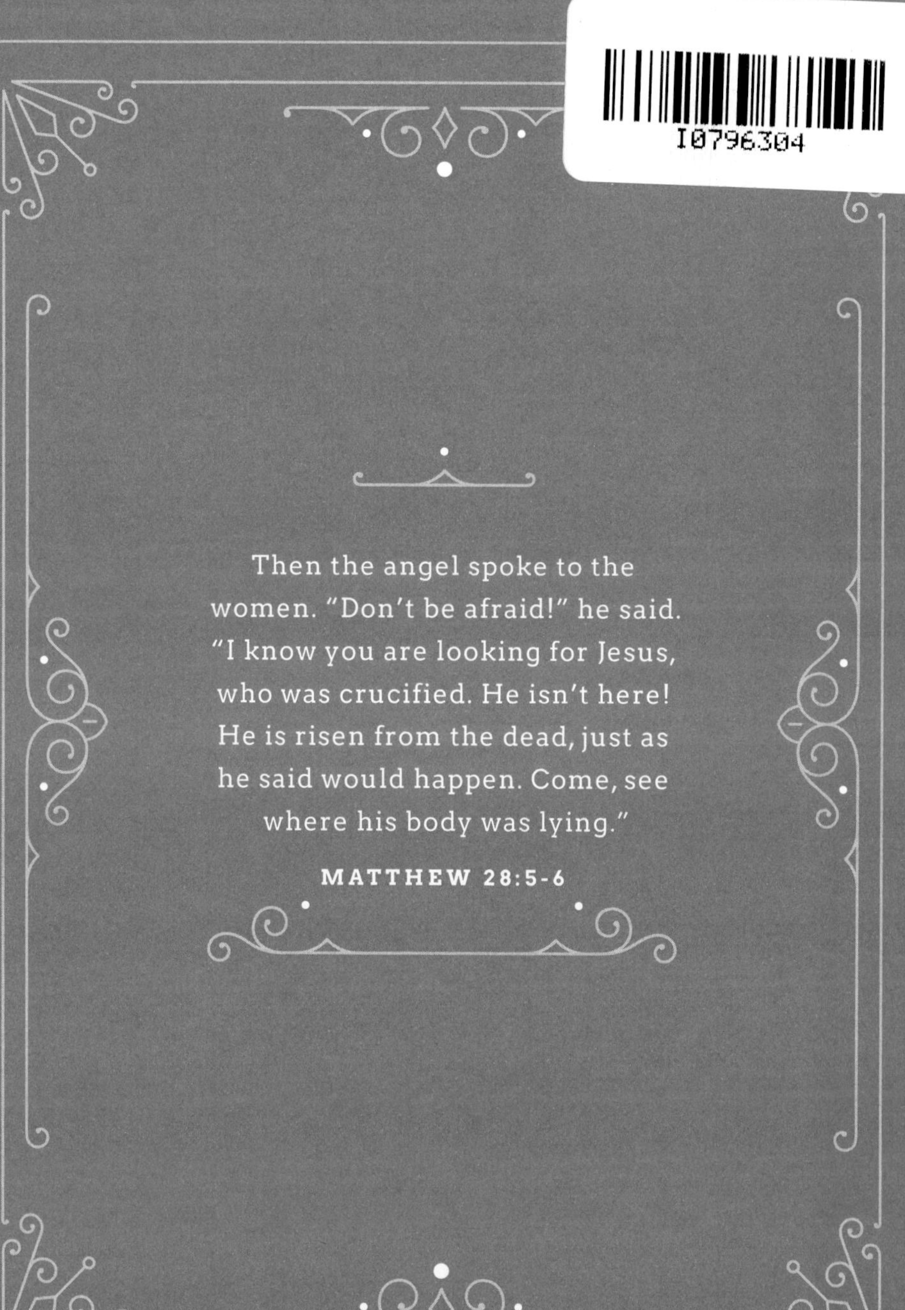

Then the angel spoke to the women. "Don't be afraid!" he said. "I know you are looking for Jesus, who was crucified. He isn't here! He is risen from the dead, just as he said would happen. Come, see where his body was lying."

MATTHEW 28:5-6

Embrace the Holy Rhythms of the Lenten Season

SACRED & STILL

JULIE FISK • KENDRA ROEHL • KRISTIN DEMERY

A Tyndale nonfiction imprint

Visit Tyndale online at tyndale.com.

Visit Tyndale Momentum online at tyndalemomentum.com.

Tyndale, Tyndale's quill logo, *Tyndale Momentum*, and the Tyndale Momentum logo are registered trademarks of Tyndale House Ministries, registered in the United States of America. Tyndale Momentum is a nonfiction imprint of Tyndale House Publishers, Carol Stream, Illinois.

Sacred and Still: Embrace the Holy Rhythms of the Lenten Season

Cover design by Eva M. Winters

Interior design by Cathy Miller

Edited by Donna L. Berg

For information about special discounts for bulk purchases, please contact Tyndale House Publishers at csresponse@tyndale.com, or call 1-855-277-9400.

ISBN 978-1-4964-8752-0

Printed in China

31 30 29 28 27 26 25
8 7 6 5 4 3 2

This book is dedicated to our kids, whose mere presence incited our spiritual curiosity and growth. May you, too, pursue Jesus with all your heart, soul, mind, and strength.

Contents

Introduction

MY FOOTSTEPS TAPPED RHYTHMICALLY across the black-and-white, geometric-patterned floor as I (Kristin) stepped directly into the choir area of the cathedral. I followed a friend to the side to slip into a row lit with small lamps. Immediately, my head tilted upward to take in the gorgeous fifteenth-century, chancel-vaulted ceiling with pendants linked in a beautiful starry pattern. A sweeping glance around the interior revealed soaring arches, stained glass windows, and various monuments.

It was my first time in an Anglican cathedral, although this one doubled as the college chapel for Christ Church at the University of Oxford in England. I was nineteen and on my first solo trip overseas for a semester at Keble College, and I wanted to soak in the history and culture of the country. Attending Evensong seemed like just one more experience I could take in.

We sat quietly on wooden seating during the procession of one of the robed choirs. As the organ notes waned, I settled in for the greeting, and then the sixteen boys of the choir began to sing soulfully, cowlicks askew, as their twelve adult counterparts filled out the rest of the swelling sound.

I sat spellbound, taking in the atmosphere, the harmony of voices, the traditions, and the liturgy. It was beautiful, serene—and entirely new for me.

You see, my sister Kendra and I grew up mainly in nondenominational churches. The desire to seek the presence of God was just as earnest in those churches as it was in this place, and yet the mantle of tradition and history added a weight that was unfamiliar to me. I wondered, *In my search for God, what else had I missed?*

It's not that I thought my experience at Evensong that night was any better or worse than the churches I'd always known and loved. Still, something about being in a place that had stood for hundreds of years and seen thousands of worshipers pad across its floors resonated deep inside me.

That experience lit an appreciation for the parts of Christianity I'd overlooked, and years later, it inspired me to experience for myself the significance of Lent.

I (JULIE) GREW UP IN A DENOMINATION that observed Lenten traditions. I remember my church's deeply meaningful liturgical rhythms throughout Lent and my own somber reflections as I fasted and prayed, even as a child, on Christ's teaching, suffering, and ultimate sacrifice. Reflective pausing in prayer and preparation for Holy Week, Good Friday, and Resurrection Sunday is a tradition we can all embrace, no matter our denominational background and subcultures.

While some denominations have specific traditions around Lent, as followers of Christ, we have freedom to observe Lent in ways that speak specifically to us as individuals and families.

This knowledge and freedom brought the three of us together several years ago to begin observing Lent as individuals and families. It was a simple idea: Each week leading up to Easter, we would pick a concern in our world to pray for, a country and people group affected by the issue, and one thing we could give up that week to remind us of others' needs.

Throughout the six weeks of Lent, we would talk with our kids about circumstances happening worldwide and even within our communities. We would pray for the needs of others, fast, and—when appropriate—find ways to give or otherwise bless others.

It became a meaningful time of year for each of us and ultimately grew into the devotional guide you now hold in your hands. Based on our own experiences and musings, we've included forty-seven daily readings to guide you through the Lenten season from Ash Wednesday to Resurrection Sunday. You'll also find suggested fasting exercises for each week throughout Lent.

Our prayer for you as you embark on this study is that you would find it as powerful as we have for awakening your heart to the true significance of the season and that you would develop your own Lenten traditions to carry on throughout the years.

Kristin, Julie, and Kendra

How to Use This Devotional

THIS BOOK EMBRACES an intentional rhythm based on weekly themes. Each Sunday sets up the theme and the fasting activity for the week. Then the devotionals from Monday through Friday are a deep dive into the theme. Saturday wraps up the week and invites you to spend time in prayerful reflection.

Whether you read one day or all forty-seven days, our hope is that you will be challenged and encouraged by each week's topic and fast. If you fall behind in the reading or break your fast, that's okay! You've got a new week, a new fast, and a fresh start every Sunday.

Ash Wednesday through Saturday: This short week sets us up for the weekly rhythm by focusing on *pursuit*—God's pursuit of us and our pursuit of him.

Sunday: This day introduces the week's theme and fast. In the appendix, you'll also find a Breath Prayer for each week to help keep you focused throughout the day.

Monday through Friday: Each day, you'll find a Scripture verse, story, prayer, question for reflection, "Sacred Rhythms" action step, and space for journaling.

Saturday: Finish the week with reflection questions designed to help you review what you've experienced and learned.

Silent Saturday and Resurrection Sunday: We break from our weekly pattern with full devotions on these two significant days.

WEEK 1

PURSUIT

Ash Wednesday–Saturday

DAY 1

God's Pursuit of Us

Long ago the LORD said to Israel: "I have loved you, my people, with an everlasting love. With unfailing love I have drawn you to myself."

JEREMIAH 31:3

"ADAM? EVE? WHERE ARE YOU?"

I (Kendra) can hear God calling to them in the garden as they hid behind the bushes, ashamed. They had never experienced such a feeling before. Even after showing themselves, they still wanted to hide, blaming others to cast aside any guilt of their own. They were attempting to cover their shame, but they also cut off their hearts from the intimacy they once shared with God. This was the first time humans tried to hide from him, but it wouldn't be the last. Sin entered the world through Adam and Eve's actions, and now we certainly know shame and guilt in many of the same ways.

Believing lies about God, ourselves, others, and the world around us, we cling to what we hope will give us peace, security, and love, realizing too late that many of those things simply leave us still lacking. We fall into sin that promises comfort and ease, only to find ourselves bound to selfish desires and lusts of the flesh that don't really fulfill our God-given purpose or desires. We are left hiding parts of ourselves from God, not wanting him to see the bits and pieces we'd rather undo or wish away. We, too, hide ashamed.

And yet.

That wasn't the end of Adam and Eve's story, and it won't be the end of ours either. As you read through the Old Testament, you'll find instances time and time again of God pursuing people. His longing for an intimate relationship is evident, his love clearly expressed, his desire to draw all people to himself plainly stated. He called throughout the ages, "I have loved you, my people, with an everlasting love. With unfailing love I have drawn you to myself" (Jeremiah 31:3).

But he has never been completely understood by humans—not in the fullness that he desired. He has been seen only as if through unclear glasses, darkly. His complete heart for all people has remained shrouded. Filtered through an imperfect humanity, his attributes as a loving God have been at times distorted and unknown. Those who were his ambassadors on earth often missed the essential parts of who he is, mistaking them at best and misrepresenting them at worst. They put heavy burdens of rules and regulations on people, which God never meant for us to have. Maybe we thought his love, his desire for us, was too good to be true. Or perhaps we knew we'd made mistakes and felt we deserved pain and strife. Maybe we didn't think we were worthy.

Regardless, this is where Jesus entered the story. Fully human. Fully God.

He arrived here as a baby, growing in all the ways every human does, and yet living a perfect life. He came to show us who God is. Who he has always been. He came to make him clearly known.

And he came to teach us how to live and how to love, paving a way back to the Father who never stopped pursuing us.

Now we see in Jesus that God did not come just for one group of people but for all of us.

> In the land of Zebulun and of Naphtali,
> beside the sea, beyond the Jordan River,
> in Galilee where so many Gentiles live,
> the people who sat in darkness
> have seen a great light.
> And for those who lived in the land where death casts its shadow,
> a light has shined.
>
> MATTHEW 4:15-16

A light shined for all of us who sat in darkness, Jew and Gentile alike. Jesus came to redeem and restore. To forgive sin and heal the diseased. To love the unlovable and the unclean, and those of us who sit in the shame of our sins, hiding ourselves from God.

Jesus came to pursue us, once again, but this time as a human so that we could touch, feel, and hear him speak clearly. Although sin was still present on earth, God chose to walk again with us.

Some call this day Ash Wednesday, putting ashes on their foreheads to signify repentance. But I think those ashes are also a beautiful picture of our humanity, of our mortality. Scripture tells us that from dust we came, and to dust we will return (see Genesis 3:19). This is worth remembering. We are nothing, and yet we are everything to God.

As we start making our way through the Lenten season, we remember God's pursuit of us. We come, ready to be fully known, fully loved, just as we are. No more hiding. No more shame. We step out from behind the bushes and call back to God, "Here I am!"

And he comes to us, running as a Father to his children, ready to embrace us and to love us. Nothing forced or coerced, just a simple welcome. All we have to do is allow ourselves to be welcomed back into the place that was always meant to be our home.

With God's help, we will respond to his promise for each of us: "Look, God's home is now among his people! He will live with them, and they will be his people. God himself will be with them" (Revelation 21:3).

Heavenly Father, thank you for pursuing humanity from the very beginning. Thank you that you never change but have always remained the same. You are continuously loving us and calling us to a relationship with yourself. We're so grateful you sent Jesus, who wholly encompasses your nature and shows us clearly who you are and have always been. Thank you for showing us, as your followers, how to live on the earth. Transform us to look more like you over these next several weeks. We love you. Thank you for loving us. Amen.

For Reflection:

How has God pursued you in the past, and how is he still pursuing you today?

Sacred Rhythms:

Now that you've had time to think about it, write down several ways God has pursued you and thank him for each one.

DAY 2

Pursuing an Intimate Relationship with God

You must love the L*ORD your God with all your heart,*
all your soul, all your mind, and all your strength.

MARK 12:30

LET ME TELL YOU ABOUT MY FRIEND: She is among the first to help—a meal dropped off, a texted prayer, a bouquet of celebratory flowers, a cup of your favorite coffee on a hard day. She is smart about how our bodies work (and don't) and shares her knowledge freely, always happy to talk about immunity, gut health, better sleep, and stress management. She is beautiful, inside and out. And those slight crinkles around her eyes that she'll lament about? They reveal her love of laughter. She is a woman of substance and faith, and I (Julie) am blessed to have her in my life.

She sounds lovely, doesn't she? Here's my point: You know *about* my friend, but you don't *know* my friend. You don't even know her name, and chances are good that you've never met her. Your knowledge of her is filtered through my perspective, meaning that you know my version of this woman based on the facts I've shared or omitted (intentionally or not).

The same goes for God. We can know *of* God. We can listen to a lifetime of sermons. We can read a library of books about who he is (or isn't). We can know the basic outline of his story. Don't get me wrong; it's valuable to read books and listen to sermons about him! But unless we are regularly pursuing a one-on-one relationship with him through prayer, worship, and reading of Scripture (the Word of God), we risk knowing *of* him rather than *knowing* him. And when we rely solely on others to tell us about him, we know only their version, their perspective of God.

No matter whether we have been a follower of Jesus for one day or one hundred years, no matter how many good deeds and faith-filled tasks we have completed, no matter how knowledgeable and mature we are in our faith, we are called into an intimate, personal relationship with God.

It's the same as any intimate relationship—parent, child, best friend, or spouse. We can skate by for a while on the foundation of our relationship and past investments of time, attention, and affection. But to maintain the strength and closeness of the connection, we need ongoing investment. If we neglect spending time and cultivating affection, the relationship suffers strain and grows distant, until we find ourselves saying things like "I thought I knew her," "I don't feel like I know him anymore," or "We've grown apart." With fellow humans, this requires an investment from both parties, so strained or lost relationships may be beyond our ability to fix. But with God, we are the ones who grow distant, not him.

In the book of Revelation, John writes letters to seven churches based on a vision he received from Jesus. The letters are Jesus' words to those particular churches, but they are instructional for us and our church communities today. Jesus commends the church in Ephesus for many things, but then he says, "I have this complaint against you. You don't love me or each other as you did at first! Look how far you have fallen! Turn back to me and do the works you did at first. If you don't repent, I will come and remove your lampstand from its place among the churches" (Revelation 2:4-5).

It should not surprise us that, just as we invest in our earthly relationships, we must be intentional about our relationship with God. And Jesus' rebuke to the church in Ephesus is comforting as I realize that I am not the only one who sometimes neglects intimacy with God—or who confuses *doing* for God with *intimacy* with God. My conversations with other followers of Christ also confirm that I am not alone in this. It's easy to get so busy serving faithfully that we neglect intimacy.

The beautiful thing about intimacy with God is that there is no need to pretend. There is no need for keeping up appearances, for trying to impress, or for being anything other than who we are. It is freeing to be nothing more and nothing less than the truest version of myself before God, even as he calls me toward growth and continued maturity.

How do we maintain (or regain) intimacy with God? We're told to go back to *first things*. And while your first things may look slightly different from mine, our spiritual foundation must consist of prayer, worship, and Scripture reading—all three of which build a love of God, involving all our heart, soul, mind, and strength.

Prayer is a cornerstone in our relationship with God. We are told to be bold, diligent, and continually in prayer (see Matthew 7:7; Luke 21:36; Romans 12:12; Ephesians 6:18). For some, prayer involves stilling our whole body in singular concentration; for others, it involves writing or journaling; and for still others, it's often done while our body is busy with a mundane task such as laundry, washing dishes, going on a walk, or driving the car. There is no "right" way to go about the process of prayer, as long as we are in regular conversation with God.

While we often think of *worship* as music because that is a common format both in Scripture and in our churches, it's really about acknowledging the goodness and sovereignty of God in and through everything we do (see Colossians 3:17). Worship is not reserved for Sunday mornings or Wednesday evenings; it's woven all throughout our days as we move through God's creation with appreciation and thanksgiving.

God uses *Scripture* to encourage, teach, refine, and grow us in our faith (see 2 Timothy 3:16). We never arrive at a point that the Word of God is no longer instructive or relevant. Our time spent in Scripture guides our days and helps us become (and remain) disciples of Jesus (see Psalm 119:105; Matthew 4:4).

The ways you and I weave prayer, worship, and Scripture into our daily rhythms will likely look different, and that's okay. The key is not to get so busy going about the work of God that we become like those in Ephesus, forgetting our first things.

Heavenly Father, thank you for calling us back into intimacy with you. Thank you for grace and a fresh start as we find a rhythm in returning to first things. Meet us as we draw near to you for the first or the millionth time with encouragement and instruction for this season. Amen.

For Reflection:

Of the three "first things" in your relationship with God—prayer, worship, and Scripture reading—which is the hardest for you to weave into your day? Which is the easiest? Why?

Sacred Rhythms:

Create a plan for finding moments of worship and prayer throughout the day, and set aside specific time to read your Bible—either through an app or a print copy.

DAY 3

Chasing Sunsets

The heavens proclaim the glory of God. The skies display his craftsmanship. Day after day they continue to speak; night after night they make him known. They speak without a sound or word; their voice is never heard. Yet their message has gone throughout the earth, and their words to all the world. God has made a home in the heavens for the sun.

PSALM 19:1-4

I (KRISTIN) EXITED THE GROCERY STORE at a brisk clip, but my pace stuttered then slowed as I noticed the sky's brilliance. Luminous pinks and oranges painted the sky in exquisite hues my camera could never do justice.

"You should go look outside," I texted my daughter once I reached the car. "The clouds are pink and pretty over by the sunset." By the time I arrived home a few minutes later, she was stepping outside our front door, head tilted upward. But other homes and large trees concealed the view.

For a second, I considered the groceries sitting in the back seat, then rolled down my window.

"Hop in," I said. Shoeless, she raced to the passenger side and buckled in. We cruised west until we hit a country road with nothing to obscure the matchless view. We paused, watching the sun's final rays disappear toward the horizon.

My daughter loves chasing beauty, especially if it's in the sky. Thanks to her, I've found myself noticing it more frequently. She's good at looking up and appreciating the sunrise, the sunset, or the clouds. In fact, if you scroll through her camera roll, that's what you'll see: Scattered among silly candid photos with friends and screenshots of cute celebrities are loads more of the sky in all its beauty—dreamy puffs of white gently scudding across the sky or angry thunderheads lumbering hugely in the distance, pearlescent gray and blue clouds juxtaposed with hues of soft yellow and gentle peach, bright rays of blinding sunlight streaming through gaps in the clouds, or misty fog rising gently from below to envelop the view.

As humans, we're wired to chase beauty. Some of it is superficial. We focus on clothes or makeup, youthfulness or strength. We marvel at a shimmering outdoor pool or an immaculate backyard, the newest decor or the fanciest homes.

But our need for the beauty provided by nature is more profound. In some ways, we are made to crave it: Our bodies revel in the vitamin D provided by the sun, and research has repeatedly demonstrated how nature positively affects our mental health.

But all this proves is that our bodies reflect an essential truth ingrained in us—that our search for beauty in all its forms is a search for the divine, and it's through creation that we glimpse it. The fingerprints of our Creator are scattered over every mountain, forest, desert, and prairie, and they all point us back to him.

In this regard, science echoes Scripture. In a paper published in the *Journal of Environmental Psychology*, researchers explored how humans respond to "ephemeral phenomena." They found that sunrises and sunsets could "trigger significant boosts in people's feelings of awe"—something that is usually hard for scientists to elicit in their research. Awe, they found, can potentially "improve mood, enhance positive social behavior, and increase positive emotions."[1]

As Christians, we know that the awe we experience over the sun's beauty isn't simply because of the colorful display. Psalm 19 talks about how the heavens are a sign of God's craftsmanship. They display his glory for us. A sunset is a wordless wonder for us to appreciate, pointing us back to him.

In this way, our pursuit of beauty becomes a turnabout. We realize that the beauty of this world is part of God's pursuit of us. He is drawing us to him. He is present in the natural world; he is there in creation because it is his. And we are his too. As children of God, we are created in the image of our Father. He is the one who created the heavens, the earth and its contents, and us, and called it all good. Because of him, we can comprehend the pleasure of the sun's warm rays on our faces or the sand between our toes. He created us that way.

The truth is that when we pursue God, we find that he is already present. When we pause to take in an awe-inspiring sunset, we can take comfort in the larger truth it reminds us of: God's glory is on display for all to see, if we'll only take the time to notice it.

And there is a steadiness to God's pursuit that is echoed in nature. The sun rises and sets every day, whether or not we notice it. God's glory is on display, reminding us that God is the same yesterday, today, and forever. He is unchanging. He is steady. Immovable. Through creation, God is writing a message to humanity that remains the same: He is always ready, always waiting, boundless and eternal. But it's up to us to see creation for what it is—an invitation into the larger story he is writing, one in which humanity chases beauty and instead finds the God who created it.

Lord, thank you for the beauty of sunrises, sunsets, and everything you have created. May we take time to notice the beauty of the world around us today, using every glimpse of beauty as an opportunity to draw closer to you. May our awe for something as simple as a sunset remind us how awesome you are, how much you love us, and how—when we pursue you—we realize that you have been waiting for us all along. Amen.

For Reflection:

How does creation remind us of God's pursuit of us? Why do you think God uses his creation to draw us to him?

Sacred Rhythms:

Spend time today watching the sunrise or the sunset. Thank God for the way in which creation reminds us of how he pursues us.

DAY 4

He Meets Us in the Moment

The Word became human and made his home among us. He was full of unfailing love and faithfulness. And we have seen his glory, the glory of the Father's one and only Son.

JOHN 1:14

SOMETIMES, WE STRUGGLE TO SEE JESUS as having been fully human. Fully God, yes. But human?

Did he feel that irrational flash of anger that swells in us when we accidentally stub our toe? Did he belly laugh at his brother's corny jokes? Was he annoyed—even momentarily—when his friends woke him up from a well-deserved nap to calm the storm? Did he ever long to be home with his family after spending so many nights on the road during his ministry?

In truth, it's easier for me (Kristin) to see him as God despite his human form. I think that's why I love the story of Lazarus so much.

It's not because Lazarus died and Jesus brought him back to life, although that is an amazing miracle. No, what I love most is Jesus' response to Lazarus's sisters, Mary and Martha. Jesus had been delayed in returning to Bethany, and by the time he returned, Lazarus was dead. Even though Jesus already knew this and intended to raise Lazarus back to life, when Martha and then Mary confronted him, he was deeply moved. Some translations say he was troubled, while others say he was angry. The Amplified Bible explains it in perhaps the most comprehensive way: "When Jesus saw her sobbing, and the Jews who had come with her also sobbing, He was deeply moved in spirit [to the point of anger at the sorrow caused by death] and was troubled" (John 11:33, AMP).

He was so moved, in fact, that he responded by weeping.

As someone who has often felt the vulnerability of crying in front of others—even when I'd rather not—I appreciate this visible demonstration of Jesus' humanity. Nothing can convince me of his humanity more readily than the fact that when he saw someone in great pain, he responded with tears of his own. Even though Jesus knew how the situation would end, he met his friends in the moment. He responded to their grief with compassion. Another version of John 11:33 says that Jesus "groaned in the spirit" (NKJV). Jesus lamented with his friends, and he laments with us when we experience the fullness of life's sorrows. Fully God, fully man.

While the passion and Easter demonstrate the fullness of Jesus as God and Savior, Lent reminds us of his humanity. As with Jesus' encounter with Mary and Martha, even though we know how the story ends—that Jesus rose again—he meets us in our moment of sorrow over his suffering and death for us. And in doing so, he draws us back to himself.

Lent is a time of preparation. It's a period in which we practice giving up or sacrificing one thing in pursuit of something even better. It's not merely a season of self-denial; it's a softening of our hearts that turns us back to God. It's only because of Lent that we're ready for the celebration of Easter.

Only through the life, death, and resurrection of Jesus can we begin to comprehend the nature of God's pursuit of us.

All of this began when the Word—that is, Jesus—became flesh and "made his home among us" (John 1:14). A home is a permanent dwelling place, not a waypoint or a rest area on the side of the road. It suggests comfort, ease, and security. Though he was God, Jesus took his place among us seriously. But, of course, he was meant for more than simply dwelling alongside humanity. The prophet Isaiah, in talking about the Messiah to come, framed it this way:

> For a child has been born—for us!
>   the gift of a son—for us!
> He'll take over
>   the running of the world.
> His names will be: Amazing Counselor,
>   Strong God,
> Eternal Father,
>   Prince of Wholeness.
> His ruling authority will grow,
>   and there'll be no limits to the wholeness he brings.
>
> ISAIAH 9:6-7, MSG

By definition, our human nature has limitations. Our bodies need air to survive, water to drink, and food to sustain us. We cannot survive subzero or sweltering temperatures without taking shelter.

But God has no such limitations, and through Jesus, he brings that limitlessness to us—not, as people thought, as an earthly ruler but as a champion of grace, an endless expanse of mercy, a fathomless well of love. As Isaiah says, there are no limits to the wholeness he brings. Only Jesus can bind our wounded hearts, soothe our fears, and inspire hope for the future. There are no limits to his mercy, grace, love, compassion, forgiveness, and power—he was and is and is to come.

Though our pursuit of God benefits us, the relentlessness of his love, grace, and mercy means that he meets us in the moment, whenever and wherever that may be. And he does so with the full knowledge of what it is to be human, just as we are.

Lord Jesus, thank you for meeting us in the moment—today and every day. During this Lenten season, may we be reminded not only of the reality of who you are as a divine God but also of the truth that you were fully human. Thank you for loving us. May we use the next few weeks to soften our hearts and be drawn to you as Savior, Lord, and friend. Amen.

For Reflection:

How does Jesus' status as both fully God and fully man impact your understanding of Lent, the passion, and Easter? In what ways can you see both the limitations of humanity and the limitlessness of his divine nature?

Sacred Rhythms:

As you walk through the next several weeks, notice your humanity—including your flaws, imperfections, and mistakes—but give yourself grace in all you observe. Let Jesus meet you in those moments, knowing he understands and wants to face each instance by your side.

WEEK 2

LOVE

Sunday–Saturday

DAY 5

The Sanctuary of God's Love

That according to the riches of his glory he may grant you to be strengthened with power through his Spirit in your inner being, so that Christ may dwell in your hearts through faith—that you, being rooted and grounded in love, may have strength to comprehend with all the saints what is the breadth and length and height and depth, and to know the love of Christ that surpasses knowledge, that you may be filled with all the fullness of God.

EPHESIANS 3:16-19, ESV

FOR MANY YEARS, my back porch was a dusty space where pollen collected on the screens and wasps magically appeared every spring. Though we had outdoor furniture, there were some years when we didn't even bother removing the dustcovers during the hot summer months because no one chose to sit there. It was an unused, unloved space.

Last year, we added a door from the main house and renovated the space into a four-season porch. We kept most of the windows but added a beautiful fireplace. Now, this once-overlooked space is where I (Kristin) spend a lot of time reading, writing, and working. From one of our swivel chairs, I have a bird's-eye view of our backyard and the trees beyond it. I can listen to the frogs in the wetlands in the spring or cozy up to the fire when snow falls in the winter. It's my sanctuary.

In our common vernacular, a "sanctuary" is a place of refuge and peace. It's also the name for the room in a church or temple where people worship—the holiest of holy places. Historically, fugitives or debtors could even find asylum in these places, taking temporary refuge and avoiding arrest.

In the Old Testament, the sanctuary was a place that God told Moses to build for him, which served as a dwelling place for God: "Let them make me a sanctuary, that I may dwell in their midst" (Exodus 25:8, ESV). Animals were sacrificed in sanctuary services as a way for people to atone for their sins. In the Old Testament sanctuary, a tabernacle (tent) included an outer room (the "Holy Place"), which was separated by a veil from an inner room (the "Most Holy Place"). Only a high priest could enter the inner room, and only once a year.

But the sanctuary took on a different format when Jesus came to earth to save us from our sins. In our new covenant with Jesus, we face a new reality: "Christ has entered, not into holy places made with hands, which are copies of the true things, but into heaven itself, now to appear in the presence of God on our behalf" (Hebrews 9:24, ESV). In other words, with Jesus at the right hand of God interceding on our behalf, we no longer need to enter the sanctuary to find forgiveness and restoration. He sacrificed his body as our High Priest once and for all. Now, God's dwelling place is not in a separate building but within us, as Paul reminds us: "Do you not know that you are God's temple and that God's Spirit dwells in you?" (1 Corinthians 3:16, ESV).

You and I need not go to a special room or even leave our house to access Jesus. It's by God's grace—rooted and grounded in love—that we are filled with the fullness of God through the Holy Spirit.

Now, God's love is our true sanctuary, providing the refuge we need. On quiet days, he offers contented rest. On days when we feel unmoored, he's our anchor. When we crave peace, he reminds us that we have all we need in him. When we're at the end of our rope, he's our lifeline.

With Christ in our hearts, we have access to the Most High God. We can enter his presence daily, hourly, or even in every moment. This week, let's find the rest our souls need in the sanctuary provided by God's love.

This Week's Fasting Focus

Give others the gift of presence this week. Just as we have benefited from the sanctuary of God's love and can access his presence anytime, anywhere, let's resolve to give others greater access to our attention. Let's be their safe space, their refuge, or even simply a source of love.

To do so, we'll fast from the constant stream of entertainment and distraction provided by our phones, televisions, or social media accounts. Practically, perhaps this means deleting social media apps from your phone for the week or setting strict usage limits. Maybe it means putting aside your work emails at a specific time of day to give others your full attention. Perhaps it means playing a game or going for a walk with people you love instead of watching a show or scrolling social media. Write down your plan and then share it with a friend or family member as an added level of accountability.

Jesus, thank you for demonstrating your love and presence by example. Thank you for allowing us to find our sanctuary in you. May we do the same for others, becoming a soft place for them to land when they need an extra dose of love or care. Help us show up for those around us this week by setting aside distractions so that we can focus on what truly matters—loving God and others. In your name, we pray. Amen.

DAY 6

God *Is* Love

God is love, and all who live in love live in God, and God lives in them.

1 JOHN 4:16

"I JUST WANT THEM TO GO to a Christian treatment center, Kendra," a concerned family member mentioned to me as we discussed a loved one caught in the throes of addiction on top of mental health issues. "I'm concerned they won't get the help they really need if they go somewhere else."

I nodded in understanding. "But if that's not what they want, and there's another program that fits their needs, I think we should support them. Even if the program isn't labeled 'Christian.'"

"But you can't find healing apart from Jesus."

"True," I said. "But I've looked at the program they're interested in, and there is support for faith traditions if the person wants it, and their therapeutic approaches are ones I'm familiar with as being effective."

The person changed the subject, and we discussed other things, but something about the exchange bothered me.

The following day, as I sat with my coffee and with my Bible open in my lap, I still couldn't shake that conversation. I read 1 John 4:16: "God is love, and all who live in love live in God, and God lives in them."

"God is love," I repeated out loud to no one in particular.

My husband, Kyle, looked up from his own reading.

"What are you thinking about?" he asked.

"Just the conversation I had yesterday. I get it—there is comfort in knowing your loved one is going to a place with 'Christian' on the doorpost. But that doesn't mean we can't find healing elsewhere. Because, really, is there any healing apart from God? Any love? Any peace?"

Kyle nodded. "Go on."

"I just remember when I worked as a therapist at the VA hospital's mental health and chemical dependency program," I continued. "There were veterans who found healing, who found peace in that place. There were also spiritual services available to everyone, and many took advantage of them. Either way, we structured our therapeutic techniques on what I believe is the truth of God's Word, even if it was never spoken out loud or acknowledged. People found healing because the approach was based on truth."

"You sound frustrated."

It was my turn to nod. "I think I am a little bit, because I feel like we limit God. We limit his power when we fail to recognize him at work in all places, even those that don't necessarily acknowledge him. Would it bother me if our family member went somewhere that was 'Christian'? Of course not, but if they're unwilling to do that, but would go to another place, why would we be upset about that?"

"I don't think we should be," Kyle agreed.

"All I know is there was love in those places I worked even though they weren't necessarily labeled 'Christian.' And I believe God was there because he is love, and we can't find real love apart from him. We miss so much of God when we don't see him in all parts of our lives and in the lives of those around us."

Love originates with God, not simply because he offers it in word and action, but because he *is* love. He is the source of all love, and there is no love apart from him.

Of course, he would love nothing more than for us to know and acknowledge his love, to relate to him and commune with him. He wants a relationship with us. There is no question that this is his ultimate desire.

But even when we don't acknowledge and commune with him, even when others don't, he still loves. Nothing diminishes his all-consuming love. It is just as present when it is recognized as being from God as when it is not.

How can we be so sure?

> When we were utterly helpless, Christ came at just the right time and died for us sinners. Now, most people would not be willing to die for an upright person, though someone might perhaps be willing to die for a person who is especially good. *But God showed his great love for us by sending Christ to die for us while we were still sinners.*
>
> ROMANS 5:6-8, EMPHASIS ADDED

Christ died for us while we were sinners. When we didn't understand our need for him or were running away from him. When we were utterly helpless. God, in his great love, sent his Son so we might know that God is love and that his redemption is near. He wanted us to know that he desires nothing more than to be in right relationship with us.

He wants us to know him as love. And once we do, we can be different. We'll *want* to be different—whole, healthy, healed. Maybe not perfectly, but with the hope of love in our lives, the old is gone and the new has come.

But God's love isn't just something to be felt. It shows up in the *action* of sending his Son, who chose to die for us so that we might know how far God would truly go for us, how deeply his love runs for us.

God fully embodies what love is—in feeling, in word, and in deed.

And that is powerful—the most powerful force the world has ever known. There is nothing greater than love. Hate can't withstand it, and neither can war, destruction, or disease. Each of these will someday crumble before the all-encompassing love of God. Love truly does win over any force of evil.

Love shows up as kindness, gentleness, mercy, peace, self-control, joy, forgiveness, empathy, and grace.

And wherever we find love in our world now—true, abiding love—we can be sure God is there. Because that's who he *is*. There is no other source of love but him. Thanks be to God, his love never ends.

Lord, help us today to see, know, and experience your love. If we've doubted or wondered how much you love us, may we come to an understanding of your love today. Please help us to know it, deep in the core of our being. Show us where you have loved us well. Open our eyes to see your goodness. And thank you that your love is always available to us and to those around us, whether acknowledged or not, because you are love. Help us share the love we first received from you with those around us. We love you. Thank you for being love and for loving us. Amen.

For Reflection:

How have you experienced the love of God in your life?

Sacred Rhythms:

Share the love of God with someone else today in word and action—whether they would accept it as coming from God or not.

Wherever we find love—true, abiding love—we can be sure God is there. Because that's who he *is.* There is no other source of love but him.

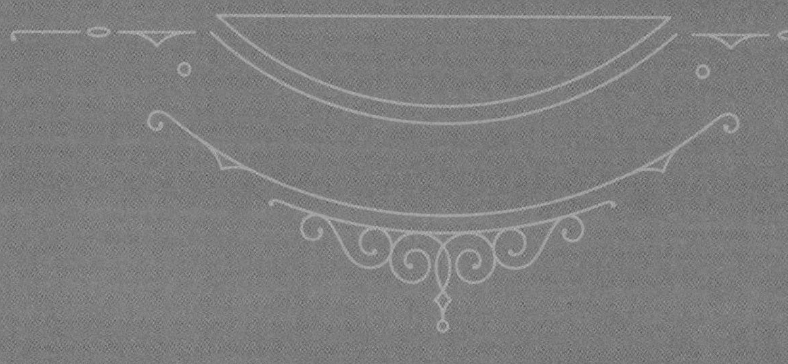

DAY 7

This Is What Love Looks Like

Love is patient and kind. Love is not jealous or boastful or proud or rude. It does not demand its own way. It is not irritable, and it keeps no record of being wronged. It does not rejoice about injustice but rejoices whenever the truth wins out. Love never gives up, never loses faith, is always hopeful, and endures through every circumstance. Prophecy and speaking in unknown languages and special knowledge will become useless. But love will last forever!

1 CORINTHIANS 13:4-8

MY FRIEND JENNY includes a hashtag with many of her social media posts: #ThisIsWhatLoveLooksLike. I (Kristin) see it when she posts about dinner with close friends, a former student she mentored in youth ministry, a collective of women choosing to give money to a local woman struggling with a cancer diagnosis, her daughter's first day of school, a man's testimony about his freedom from addiction, her family's fluffy dog, a shopping trip with her nieces, outings with friends, her work with a breakfast club ministry, and holidays with family.

But it's not just about the activities and events she's involved in; it's what she says about the people in her posts. She's celebrating friends for their successes, their uniqueness, or their gifts. She's calling out the good in them and speaking life into their everyday existence. She's marveling at the opportunity to witness the work of God in the world through her life and the lives of those around her. In her posts, it's clear that "this is what love looks like" is really another way of saying "this is what the love of Jesus looks like in this world."

Our perception of love can sometimes become watered down by culture and the limited nature of using a single word for a multifaceted concept. We hear throwaway comments about how we "love" pizza, pedicures, weekends, or the neighbor's cute dog. There's nothing wrong with appreciating food or foot care. Still, the sentiment misses the fierce nature of love—specifically, the love of Jesus for us and for those around us—and how life-changing and all-encompassing it really is.

Yet, Romans 12:9 reminds us, "Don't just pretend to love others. Really love them. Hate what is wrong. Hold tightly to what is good." In our attempts to authentically love others, we must keep a firm grip on the good. Love is active, and it's a choice.

But what does that look like on a practical level? Just a few verses earlier, Paul spells it out by urging us to offer our lives to God as a living, holy sacrifice. I love how *The Message* explains the concept: "Here's what I want you to do, God helping you: Take your everyday, ordinary life—your sleeping, eating, going-to-work, and walking-around life—and place it before God as an offering. Embracing what God does for you is the best thing you can do for him" (Romans 12:1, MSG).

Eating and going to work seem like the boring parts of our lives, not the parts where the good stuff happens. Yet even these can be opportunities to love others. It's love when we make and share a meal with someone else. It's also love when we listen to a coworker vent about a challenging relationship or their broken-down-car woes. We choose love when we are patient, kind, and gentle. Love doesn't give up or lose faith, and it remains hopeful and persistent despite circumstances. We choose to love when we believe the best about a friend, when we open the door for a delivery person, when we give someone the benefit of the doubt, and when we refuse to give in to road rage when an inconsiderate driver cuts us off.

The truth is that our decision to love others is most easily measured by how we choose to spend our time—our everyday, ordinary life. Just as Jesus showed love day in and day out by walking dusty roads with his disciples, sharing meals with those many considered unlovable, and writing words in the dirt that turned a woman's accusers away, love is an everyday action. Love is caring for our neighbor, choosing to listen, and being patient with our toddler. It's forgiving seventy times seven, turning our cheek, offering to share our home or a meal. It's caring for the sick, supporting orphans and widows, and treating others justly. It's volunteering with kids, dropping off homemade jam for a neighbor, or texting someone to let them know we're thinking of them. None of this is about earning God's love, of course, but rather about showing our gratitude for the way he loves us. Every day, how we spend our minutes and hours adds silent tallies that can show us where our priorities lie. We "vote" with our time. As Paul's words in Romans remind us, loving others is a way to worship Jesus. This is what love looks like.

The funny thing is that being the hands and feet of Jesus is often the way we learn the most about love and what it means to love. As with the parables Jesus used to teach us about faith and the world, demonstration is our teacher. And the stories we go on to tell others about God's work help us testify to his love.

Jesus, thank you that you offered the first and best demonstration of what love looks like. Help us to emulate you in all we do, offering our daily lives and love for others as a way to worship you. May we be your hands and feet in the world, celebrating and participating in your work on earth through us. Amen.

For Reflection:

In your daily life, what does love look like? How do you show others love? How do they show love to you?

Sacred Rhythms:

Today, use a notepad or the notes section on your phone to keep track of what love looks like in your daily life. Use your list to see where you might need to adjust your priorities.

Being the hands and feet of Jesus is often the way we learn the most about love.

DAY 8

Because He First Loved Us

We love each other because he loved us first.

1 JOHN 4:19

"I DON'T REALLY UNDERSTAND," the young man said. "Why would you want to get to know us, Kendra?"

"What do you mean?" I asked.

"Well, if I were in your situation and taking in foster kids, I'm not sure I would want to get to know the biological family. Isn't it hard?"

I paused, trying to think of what to say next.

"Yes and no," I responded. "I guess my only answer is that we have been loved. We have felt invited in as family by God. How could we not want to extend that same invitation to others? Jesus loves us. We feel like we're just giving others what we've already received."

He nodded in understanding. "I'm still amazed that you would do it."

I shrugged. "We're not perfect people. We sometimes struggle to love and be kind, but we've also just determined to try to follow Jesus, and that means inviting people, even strangers, in as family. We're glad to be here with you and your family."

His question was not an unusual one. As foster and adoptive parents, Kyle and I have gotten many comments or questions over the years about the relationship we have with our kids' biological families. And although we have established more careful boundaries with some family members to keep our kids as healthy as we can, we know it's essential for our children to know as many of their relatives as possible. We understand that kids do better when they can connect with someone from their biological families.[1]

Sometimes, that feels like a sacrifice, but mostly it feels like the right thing to do. God has given Kyle and me all of our children and family to mentor or influence, whether they are biological, adopted, step, extended, or informal. They are God's gifts to us. To raise. To love. To teach. And then to allow to fly. We hold them loosely and tightly at the same time, feeling the tension of knowing that they are entrusted to us for a time but then are meant to create their own life, a life that God has planned for each of them. They are meant to have families of their own and people to love. That includes us, certainly. But love is intended for so much more than just our own benefit. It's for anyone around us whom God would ask us to bring into our family.

And isn't that just how God meets each one of us as children that he dearly loves? He brings in those of us who are lonely, who feel unloved or unwelcome, and says, "You're welcome here. This is your home. You're a part of my family." And once you know and experience his great love, love that is never forced on us, turning from it seems unimaginable.

But God's invitation doesn't end with us. He welcomes us in and then invites us to show that same love, acceptance, and welcome to others. Life is meant to be done in community, but not just any kind of community—one as close as a family.

How can I be so sure? Ephesians 1:4-5 says, "Even before he made the world, God loved us and chose us in Christ to be holy and without fault in his eyes. God decided in advance to adopt us into his own family by bringing us to himself through Jesus Christ. This is what he wanted to do, and it gave him great pleasure."

Even before the world was made, God loved us. He chose us. He decided in advance to adopt us and call us family, bringing us into a closer union through Jesus. And it wasn't because he felt like he had to, out of some sort of duty. No. He *wanted* to welcome us in.

It brings him great pleasure to welcome you. To welcome me. To welcome each one of us.

Have you experienced that welcome?

If so, you now have the great pleasure of inviting others into the same family. If not, rest assured that his welcome is available to you right now. He is pleased to invite you into his family. That's the heart of a Father who loves his children. You can rest in that love today and every day.

His love for us is settled. There's no striving to receive it. He's already made every bit of himself available to us.

A few years after my conversation with that young man, we visited his family at their home. We learned that, along with their own small children, they were now caring for a foster child with special needs. The young man told me how God had been doing a work in his heart, and that our conversation had been just one small piece in God's calling on him and his family toward a life of welcoming others in as family.

I couldn't help but smile at the goodness of God.

It's a lesson we can all learn and grow into more and more. We truly do love because he has first loved us.

Heavenly Father, thank you for your love that pursues us. For choosing us even before the world was made. For inviting us in as family. Thank you for wanting us. May we experience your love today. When we struggle to know just how much you desire to have us be a part of your family, help us come to a greater understanding of the depth of your love for us. Help us to take time and to shut off distractions so we can experience your love anew. Then help us to welcome others the same way you've welcomed us. Give us a heart that loves others like you do. Give us a fuller understanding of where this kind of love comes from: It comes from the love we first received from you. We love you. Amen.

For Reflection:

How has God's love for you changed how you love others?

Sacred Rhythms:

Pray and ask God who around you needs to feel loved. Invite them to coffee, dinner, or some other activity.

Isn't that just how God meets each one of us? He brings in those who are lonely, who feel unloved or unwelcome, and says, "This is your home. You're a part of my family."

DAY 9

The Unexpected Gift of Loving Others

"I am giving you a new commandment: Love each other. Just as I have loved you, you should love each other. Your love for one another will prove to the world that you are my disciples."

JOHN 13:34-35

"JULIE, I AM WHO I AM and where I am, largely because of the parents of my high school best friend," Adam said, swiping a bite of tiramisu from his wife's plate before continuing. "Tara and I watch for opportunities to influence young people in the same way. It's our way of paying it forward."

Adam was the youngest child of four raised by a single dad whose job meant that he wasn't home much and when he was, he was emotionally spent. When Adam speaks of favorite childhood memories and traditions, most of his stories are about funny adventures in the homes of friends and extended family. Adam learned what stable, healthy households look like from others, especially from Donna and John, his best friend's parents. They saw Adam's situation, and without fanfare or announcement, found a multitude of ways to embrace him, love him, and help launch him into adulthood.

My husband, Aaron, and I knew generally about Adam's childhood, but his words hung in the air. The four of us—Aaron and I and Adam and Tara, all currently parents of busy teens—reconsidered Adam's story through the eyes of Donna and John, including the emotional and physical effort they had invested in a child they were not obligated to care for.

On the way home from the restaurant afterward, Aaron was the first to broach the topic of Donna and John with a quiet statement: "I want to be like them."

"I know—me too," I whispered back, even as I contemplated the moments when Donna and John surely found it inconvenient to drive back and forth across town to make Adam a part of the family fun, or when they were exhausted and cranky and yet included him in the chaos and ruckus of their home on weekends.

Thinking of my own teens and their friends, I silently prayed, *Lord, help me not love comfort more than the people you put in front of me. Help me be like Donna and John. Help me see the Adams among my teens' friends.*

And isn't that the truth of it? We want to love others, we want to be difference makers like Donna and John . . . until it's ten thirty at night and we're delivering a carload of loud middle schoolers back home while wishing we were snuggled in bed.

Loving others well almost always comes at the cost of comfort, convenience, and/or the joy of getting our preference.

Believe me, that sentence was as painful for me to type as it likely was for you to read. When I'm feeling overscheduled, when I am maxed out emotionally, timewise, or physically, the thought of adding even one more small thing (especially at the expense of my comfort) can feel like my carefully constructed house of cards will collapse into chaos.

But if I truly want to obey the command found in today's verse, if I want to love others as God loved me, if I want to call myself a disciple of the Lord Jesus Christ, I am called to a life of sacrificial love. And when we love like this—even imperfectly—our love will "prove to the world" that we are Jesus' disciples (John 13:35). In other words, our willingness to love sacrificially proves who we belong to: God.

In a world convinced that power comes through money, high position, or influence, those who belong to God are wielding the often quiet, always immeasurable and unstoppable power of sacrificial love. We don't need a fancy degree, a hefty balance in our bank account, a beautifully decorated house, or a certain threshold of influence to get about the work of the Father. We need simply to notice and obey.

We complicate it by placing preconditions on Jesus' command, mistakenly incorporating ideas based on the world's perspective on power. We're tempted to believe that our small obediences are too insignificant and quiet to matter, especially when they cost us comfort, convenience, or preference.

Don't believe that lie. What might have felt insignificant to Donna and John was life-changing for Adam. Each invitation, each drive across town to pick up and drop off, each meal around their table built upon one another, creating space for him within their family. Adam watched and learned through repeated proximity over time, each interaction a small part of an ordinary day in an ordinary week. And yet Adam speaks of those experiences as transformational and foundational to who he is as an adult. It's often in the ordinary, small obediences that God uses us to impact the lives of those around us.

Before you scrunch your nose at the prospect of a lifetime of lost comfort in the name of sacrificial love, consider this plot twist: We ourselves are almost always blessed in the midst of service to God through loving others. As reluctant as I might initially find myself when faced with the opportunity to love sacrificially, I often walk away from the experience with my own spiritual and emotional tanks filled to overflowing. It is in the pouring out that I myself am refilled in ways that surpass a mere day at the spa. While there is absolutely nothing wrong with visiting the spa, the rejuvenation and encouragement found in service to others as an act of loving obedience and worship to God is a spiritual refreshment that lasts far longer.

But most importantly, my sacrificial love of others is a silent but compelling reminder that I belong to God and that they can too. Our actions speak of our faith, oftentimes with more influence and power than mere words.

Heavenly Father, thank you for your unconditional, never-ending love. And thank you that the world will know us as your disciples through our love for those around us. Help us to recognize your invitations into loving service, and nudge us into obedience, even when our first desire is to decline. As we practice sacrificial love, may the world recognize us as your disciples, just as Jesus' words promise. Amen.

For Reflection:

Who are the "Adams" in your life? Prayerfully consider your various circles of community. Who is quietly struggling? Who needs a listening ear? Who needs to be welcomed into healthy community?

Sacred Rhythms:

Make a list based on your reflection, and ask God for an opportunity to show love to someone on your list.

Those who belong to God are wielding the often quiet, always immeasurable and unstoppable power of sacrificial love.

DAY 10

Building the Community We Need

If possible, so far as it depends on you, live peaceably with all.

ROMANS 12:18, ESV

I (JULIE) WAS ELBOW-DEEP in kitchen-sink suds when my fifth-grade daughter burst through our front door. Wiping my hands on a nearby towel, I moved to intercept her with a hug, but I drew up short, reading the fury in her body language from across the room.

She was fresh off the school bus, and she was furious.

"Honey, what's wrong? What happened?"

"Mom, boys fight with their fists, but girls? Girls fight with their words!"

Her indignant voice still lives in my head with that shouted-out phrase. The what and why of the story no longer matters, but the heartache over learning to navigate friendship lingers. Friendships (both casual and close) can be incredibly hard, and yet we rarely talk about the intentional effort that goes into healthy, functional relationships outside of marriage and family.

Ads and our social media feeds show us the best parts of friendships (laughter, adventures, fun nights out), but they skip over the harder moments of talking through differences, apologizing for hurtful words or actions, listening well, sitting alongside one another through grief, and staying connected through the ebb and flow of life's changing seasons.

There is an illusion that our role in relationships is passive: We will magically be invited into a community, and friendships will simply, somehow, happen to us rather than requiring us to play an active role as inviters, creators, and maintainers. And once in community and in friendships, there is an assumption that we can coast along indefinitely, that these types of relationships don't require the same level of effort and intentionality as family and spouse relationships.

Of course, those assumptions are not true. Yes, proximity, timing, and season of life play a significant role in developing new friendships and maintaining established ones. But two biblical principles (one inward and one outward focused)—when followed even imperfectly—are foundational to bringing health and vibrancy to any community of people you find yourself in: coworkers, fellow church members, neighbors, extended family, and besties.

1. **Be cautious about sharing another's story.** The book of Proverbs tells us that among the things that the Lord hates and that are an abomination to him are "a false witness who breathes out lies, and one who sows discord among brothers" (6:19, ESV).

While some secrets are dangerous and must be told, most often, people simply need a confidential sounding board, someone with a listening ear who will allow them to verbally process their experiences, who will pray alongside them, and who will—if the moment is right—gently hold them accountable.

A friend of mine worked in a place where gossip ran rampant. In response to that culture, she began intentionally zipping her lips. If it wasn't necessary to pass on information about a coworker—especially if it could cause drama—she didn't. As coworkers realized they could talk to her without their words being repeated, they sought her out for conversations around the harder parts of their lives. My friend dispensed more biblical wisdom (sometimes with Jesus' name attached and sometimes not) during her years there simply because she became a trusted listener in a space where that was rare.

When I adopted this practice (imperfectly, because this is a work in progress for me!), I was surprised to realize how much of our general conversation is about other people. Eek! Even when it isn't technically gossip, telling stories about those not in the room can quickly become a slippery slope into negative, drama-causing conversations.

As my friend found, I was amazed at how quickly that simple change in conversational behavior identifies you as a "safe person"—and at the intensely personal things others will share, and the godly wisdom that you'll be invited to dispense. This holds true not only within friendships but also in more casual community.

2. Embrace an abundance mindset. In the book of James, we read that "Where jealousy and selfish ambition exist, there will be disorder and every vile practice" (3:16, ESV).

Jealousy and envy are toxic, especially when we compare our secret worst to another's public best. With the pervasiveness of social media and celebrity, we might understand this intellectually even as our hearts still get tripped up over what we believe others have, compared to our lack.

Friends, our heavenly Father owns the cattle on a thousand hills (see

Psalm 50:10). He does not have a quota on answering prayers. His healing or financial miracle or provision of the "perfect" job for your neighbor does not exhaust or diminish his ability to take care of you or your loved one. In his abundance, there is enough for *all* of us. It sounds silly to say, but how often do we walk around with a scarcity mindset, falling into a way of thinking that leads us to act as though that is the truth—that God does *not* have enough for all of us?

Instead of ruminating on *Why her?* or *Why them?* in my own waiting seasons, I seek (again, imperfectly) to focus on recounting the answered prayers of others as evidence of God's goodness and faithfulness. I label instances of God's past faithfulness as "fingerprints," and as I pray over my situation, I remind God of his "fingerprints" in the lives of Kendra, Kristin, and others—including my past self. It's a way to bolster my faith and acknowledge his steady presence in our lives, even when it isn't always obvious. By embracing God's provision for my *friends* as evidence of his faithfulness to intercede in *my* situation, their "wins" become my "wins"—and I can rely upon both when growing my faith.

When we embrace the truth about God's ability to intercede without regard for what he is doing (or not) for someone else, when we embrace his "fingerprints" in the lives of others as evidence of his goodness and his ability to do the same for us, we shift from creating distance and division based on jealousy or envy to close community in which the goodness of God is recognized and celebrated, even as we wait.

Another friend of mine, a spiritually mature leader I admire deeply, openly shares her story of jealousy over another woman's ministry. When she took her jealousy to God, frustrated at this other woman's forward movement compared to my friend's unmet need, God asked my friend to pray for the other woman, gently reminding her that she knew nothing of this other woman's private struggle. As my friend prayed regularly in reluctant obedience, her heart softened, and her own prayers were answered.

For those of us waiting, this can be incredibly hard. Shifting our mindsets from scarcity to abundance is both countercultural and often intertwined with lament and grief. We can hold joy and lament, grief and rejoicing in equal portions. Having an abundance mindset does not mean we must deny or diminish our disappointment. But we cannot allow our grief to shift into envy. And while your friend may have that thing you are desperately praying for, it's important to understand that she has her own troubles which you may know nothing about.

Uffda. Guarding our tongues and refusing the lure of envy and jealousy are not easy tasks. Like me, you may find yourself needing to confess to falling short from time to time, asking God to forgive and to allow you an opportunity to do better. But when we embrace these biblical principles, we'll find it easier to live harmoniously and at peace with those around us.

Heavenly Father, help us be people who build and contribute to healthy communities and friendships. May we use caution in our stories, especially about those not currently in the room. May we turn to you whenever we feel the sting of envy, releasing that poison through prayer even as we embrace lament. And may we be gentle and grace-filled to those around us waiting on you, tender and empathetic to their waiting season. Amen.

For Reflection:

Which of the two friendship principles—(1) be cautious about sharing another's story, or (2) embrace an abundance mindset—is more difficult for you? Does it change depending upon your circumstances or who you are around? How do your answers provide insight for moving forward?

Sacred Rhythms:

Pick one for this week: (1) Develop one or two questions to ask or a conversational tidbit to use to avoid telling the stories of others. (2) List God's "fingerprints" in your life and in the lives of those around you. Thank God for each one.

When we embrace God's "fingerprints" in the lives of others as evidence of his goodness and his ability to do the same for us, we shift from jealousy or envy to close community.

DAY 11

For Further Reflection

1. What stood out to you about love this week? What surprised or inspired you? What tested or challenged you?

2. What insights did you gain through this week's fast from the distractions of phones, television, and social media?

3. How do you love others well, and where can you work to improve?

Lord Jesus, thank you for the gift of your love. We're grateful that your love is a place of refuge and rest for us, a sanctuary when we need it most. Help us to offer that same sense of comfort and care to others as we follow your example. Thank you for welcoming us into your family as your children. May we, in turn, do the same by seeking opportunities to invite others into our lives, our communities, and our families—even when it comes at the expense of our comfort or convenience. May we be willing to love sacrificially, obedient to doing the work of your Kingdom here on earth. Help us to have an eye toward building and contributing to a healthy community, always pointing others back to you and your love. Amen.

WEEK 3

FORGIVENESS

Sunday–Saturday

DAY 12

Healed Inside and Out

Confess your sins to one another and pray for one another, that you may be healed. The prayer of a righteous person has great power as it is working.

JAMES 5:16, ESV

SEVERAL YEARS AGO, I (Kristin) heard about an interview with a woman named Mary Johnson-Roy in which she talked about her son's death and the extraordinary forgiveness she extended afterward. When her son was a young man, he and another young man named Oshea Israel got into a fight, and Oshea killed her son. Some years after Oshea was convicted of murder, Mary visited him in prison. Instead of the boy she remembered, he was now a man. She told him about her son, and he listened. She forgave him for what he'd done. Before Mary left, she began to cry, and Oshea hugged her as though she were his own mother.

After Oshea finished his sentence, he ended up living next door to Mary. Their relationship grew stronger, and they began to check in on each other and treat each other like mother and son. By the time Oshea married and had two children, he considered Mary to be their grandmother. And when Mary married later in life, Oshea walked her down the aisle.[1]

Mary and Oshea's story is a powerful example of forgiveness. It's the kind of restoration that most of us can't imagine—one that looks beyond the grievous harm and sees the humanity of the person who caused it.

At its root, forgiveness is the healing of an internal wound. It is powerful—so powerful, in fact, that only God can bring it about.

The book of Mark tells the story of a visit Jesus made to Capernaum. The news of his visit spread quickly, and the home he was staying in became so packed that there wasn't even room outside the door. As he was preaching, four men arrived with their friend, who was paralyzed. Since they could not shoulder their way inside, they dug a hole in the roof above Jesus and lowered the man down.

Seeing him, Jesus told the man his sins were forgiven—which outraged the religious leaders.

"What is he saying? This is blasphemy! Only God can forgive sins!" they thought (Mark 2:7).

The leaders didn't even need to say these words aloud for Jesus to recognize their indignation. He asked them, "Is it easier to say to the paralyzed man 'Your sins are forgiven,' or 'Stand up, pick up your mat, and walk'?" (verse 9).

With that, Jesus turned to the man and told him to take his mat and go home, which he did. Jesus demonstrated his authority to forgive sin by showing that he had the power to heal. But the man's healing inside and out illustrated the monumental nature of forgiveness. Why else would Jesus choose to forgive the man—essentially healing him inside—before also healing his exterior? Arguably, the man's ability to walk would have seemed more miraculous. Yet Jesus' priority was the man's heart, not his legs.

You and I have our own stories, different from those of Mary and Oshea, and from the paralyzed man who came down through the roof. But like them, we have sinned and need forgiveness. We have had the opportunity to deeply experience God's forgiveness and the healing and restoration that only he can give. Jesus looks past the ugly muck of our sinfulness and sees our humanity; he sees us as family members to reclaim and restore. The greater the separation, the more profound the forgiveness.

This Week's Fasting Focus

This week, we want to remind ourselves of the value of doing something *difficult* that has something *good* embedded in it—in much the same way that extending forgiveness to someone can be difficult but ultimately beneficial. So this week's fast is to forgo comfort and convenience by putting the needs of others first or putting ourselves in someone else's shoes.

On a practical level, this could include choosing a parking spot farther from a store's entrance, opening the door for someone, or letting another person go in front of you in line. Or, you could use interactions this week to put yourself in someone else's shoes. For instance, if you have a negative interaction, reflect on why—perhaps the person has a lot going on in their personal life, didn't sleep well the night before, or is battling a head cold. Choosing to give others the benefit of the doubt flexes our empathy muscles and can help us the next time we need to forgive someone else.

Jesus, thank you for the power of forgiveness to heal and restore us, inside and out. May we realize the depth of your sacrificial forgiveness, and may it remind us to do our own part. Help us to forgive ourselves and others for the many ways we've fallen short or caused harm. May we use this week as an opportunity to forgo our own comfort and convenience and see those around us with the same loving, empathetic gaze as the Father. Amen.

DAY 13

One-Sided Forgiveness

If you forgive those who sin against you,
your heavenly Father will forgive you.

MATTHEW 6:14

I (JULIE) LOVE MY FRIEND CASSIDY'S STORY of forgiveness and how it changed her life. Cassidy tells charmingly funny stories about her early childhood in a small hometown. But when you ask about her teen years, her carefully measured response speaks of the harder parts of small-town living.

The dynamics of Cassidy's friend group changed in her sophomore year with the arrival of a girl named Blake. The healed, adult version of Cassidy is gracious and gentle toward that fifteen-year-old version of Blake, even though she frequently made Cassidy feel too loud, too rural, too uncool, and simply too much. But given Blake's cool-girl popularity and a class size of only forty students, it was impossible to completely avoid or ignore her.

Cassidy shed uncountable tears over Blake's subtle (and not so subtle) snubs and ringleading of their friend group to do the same until Cassidy "escaped" to college, leaving her community and classmates for an entirely new place and a fresh start. Certain she had moved on to better things, Cassidy was surprised to realize halfway through her first semester that her stomach clenched with anxiety whenever she heard the name Blake—or any similar sounding word. While she'd physically left Blake behind, the hurt and tension clung to her, continuing to ambush her in ways and at times that were disheartening and heavy.

It wasn't until spring semester that Cassidy finally took her pain over Blake to God. One Wednesday night, weary of carrying the weight of those high school years, she chose to forgive Blake and asked Jesus to take the negative emotions that had knotted her up whenever she heard Blake's name. In the days and weeks that followed, Cassidy imagined handing Jesus her knot of anxiety every time it tried to settle upon her. She did this over and over, until it became a reflexive habit. As the stress started to build, Cassidy would immediately hand it over in prayer, reminding Jesus (and more importantly, herself) that she had already chosen forgiveness and no longer wanted to carry the pain.

The change in Cassidy was so gradual, so nuanced that she barely realized it was happening. But a year later, she heard someone shout, "Blake, wait up! I'll go to the dining hall with you." Cassidy braced for that inevitable swell of anxiety—and was surprised by her neutral reaction. No pit of anxiety. No stomach-clenching nerves. No fear of what would be mocked this time. Stunned, she stopped in the middle of a busy sidewalk to probe her feelings, and still felt . . . nothing.

That *nothing* felt light and joyous, as though a weight had been lifted that Cassidy didn't know she was carrying. So she began a new habit: Every time she heard a word that sounded like *Blake*, she would pause to enjoy the lack of a negative emotional reaction and to thank Jesus for removing that burden.

But the best part of Cassidy's story is the man she met three years later. While no marriage is perfect, she would tell you that her husband, *Blake*, has been one of the sweetest, most beautiful gifts of redemption God has bestowed upon her. Blake: the name that once induced anxiety, insecurity, and deep hurt is now the name that brings security, laughter, and love.

The thing I love about Cassidy's story is how conspicuously God used her forgiveness to exchange her years of pain for decades of joy. But I also love this story because we don't know what happened to Blake. There is no vengeance or retribution (frequent themes of comeuppance for "wrongdoers" in our culture) to revel in nor any glee to be found in Blake's own suffering. And who knows how Jesus may have intersected Blake's life; it's quite possible that adult Blake is a lovely woman who has asked to be (and been) forgiven by God and whose life now reflects a deep faith in Christ.

Forgiveness is, foremost, between us and God, and while we often talk about forgiveness in terms of the other person, the key to forgiveness is in our sole possession. We need not wait a moment longer for another person's apology. We can take our disappointment, hurt, anger, and pain to Jesus, telling him that we forgive and asking him to hold the weight of our emotions.

We are commanded to forgive. Today's verse and others (see Proverbs 17:9; Matthew 18:21-22; Colossians 3:12-13) are clear that forgiveness must be part of our identity as followers of Jesus. (Please note that a command to forgive does not mean we must stay in harmful situations or cannot establish boundaries. We can extend forgiveness while also being wise about unhealthy situations and people.)

Why are we commanded to forgive? Among many reasons, three stand out this Lenten season.

First, we forgive others to cleanse our hearts and minds from bitterness, rage, anger, harsh words, slander, and evil behavior (see Ephesians 4:31). The devil is real, and when we camp in unforgiveness, he can use these negative emotions to continue harming us—above and beyond the original hurt. Anger, when allowed to fester, is terrible for our mental and physical health, in addition to negatively impacting all of our relationships.[1]

Second, we model Jesus and the life he invites us to live (even imperfectly) when we practice forgiveness (see Ephesians 4:32). As followers of Jesus, and as new creatures in Christ, we are called to live lives that reflect the love of God to the world around us (see 2 Corinthians 5:17; Ephesians 4:24).

Third and most important, we forgive others because we ourselves need to be forgiven. I don't know about you, but I need the unmerited mercy and grace found in the forgiveness of my sins. Today's Scripture is clear: Because I need to be forgiven of my own sins, I must also be willing to forgive others. When I am unwilling to forgive, it can damage my relationship with God.

While there are other important reasons to embrace forgiveness as a life practice, it's clear that forgiveness is a critical part of our growth as followers of Jesus.

Heavenly Father, it's so easy to talk about the idea of forgiveness, and yet the reality of it is almost always incredibly difficult. Just as you did for Cassidy, walk alongside us as we continually hand you the hurt and harm, reclaiming forgiveness until our emotions catch up with our intentional choice to forgive. Give us wisdom in boundaries so that forgiveness and preventing harm can live side by side. Amen.

For Reflection:

Where have you allowed unforgiveness to fester without regard to the other person or persons?

Sacred Rhythms:

Don't let today's sun set without confessing that unforgiveness to God. Forgive and release the hurt to him.

We need not wait a moment longer for another person's apology. We can take our disappointment, hurt, anger, and pain to Jesus, asking him to hold the weight of our emotions.

DAY 14

Forgiving God

He has planted eternity in the human heart, but even so, people cannot see the whole scope of God's work from beginning to end.

ECCLESIASTES 3:11

I STOOD SILENTLY, jaw clenched, eyes screwed shut but lifted heavenward, heart pounding in brokenhearted anger as the worship song crescendoed around me. It was the sixth Sunday that I (Julie, then twenty-eight) had refused to sing, even as I stood in united, corporate worship.

Katrina Stigman, one of my best friends (and older sister to Kendra and Kristin), mother to two small children, was dead at age twenty-eight from breast cancer, and I was incandescently angry at God. This was not the way the story was supposed to go. God had answered so many prayers throughout Katrina's journey, and I just *knew* that the story of her complete healing was going to be a glorious testimony to God's miracle-working ways. Her family, her friends, and hundreds of people following her journey had prayed all the prayers. We'd believed in her healing with our whole hearts (which was far more faith than a mustard seed!). We'd done all the things all the books and miracle experts promised would unleash her final, complete healing, and still she died.

It was during the third song of my silent vigil on that sixth Sunday that I realized I had a choice to make: Either I lay my anger down before God and concede that his will is both sovereign and sometimes unfathomable this side of heaven, or I walk away from God.

So upon returning home from church, I found a quiet spot and broke my angry silence with the Lord. I shared my confusion and my disillusioned belief that bad things can't happen to faithful, praying people. I shared my heartbreak, even as I confessed his sovereignty. I told God that I chose him in that private moment with a gravity and solemnity that, to this day, feels weightier than any of my previous public declarations.

As I chose God, I whispered a prayer: *Please, Lord, please use her life, her steadfast faithfulness during cancer for your eternal glory. Allow me to speak of Katrina to others. Open doors and windows so that I might tell portions of her story to those who will never meet her, that her legacy would continue to impact eternity.*

It's been almost twenty years, and God has faithfully answered that prayer hundreds of times, starting the week after I prayed it. Kendra, Kristin, and I call Katrina our silent fourth partner, so great has her influence been in our lives and in our writing. We speak of her often and both love and miss her terribly.

In truth, it wasn't that God needed my forgiveness; it was that I'd believed twisty theology and mixed my deep grief with anger at God when I couldn't manipulate him into doing what I wanted (earthly healing for my loved one). Manipulation is a strong word, but that's what it was, even though my intentions were good. It wasn't that my audacious prayers were wrong. Jesus himself tells us to pray with boldness and persistence (see Matthew 7:7). However, the moment I believe that God must do as I ask if I say the right words or combine my praying with a "seed of faith"—often in the form of money—I'm straying into manipulation and wrong theology. And then, when my prayer isn't answered in the way I desperately want, I'm left in a crisis of faith, angry at God over my mistaken expectations amid great sorrow.

Can God's sovereignty be manipulated? Scripture is clear: no. Consider these words from the book of James: "How do you know what your life will be like tomorrow? Your life is like the morning fog—it's here a little while, then it's gone. What you ought to say is, 'If the Lord wants us to, we will live and do this or that'" (4:14-15).

Do we understand—this side of heaven—the *why* behind seemingly unanswered prayers, delays in answers to prayers, or prayers answered in ways we would not have chosen? Also no.

> For who can know the LORD's thoughts?
>   Who knows enough to give him advice?
> And who has given him so much
>   that he needs to pay it back?
>
> For everything comes from him and exists by his power and is intended for his glory. All glory to him forever! Amen.
>
> ROMANS 11:34-36

Do I understand how humanity's free will intersects with God's sovereignty as it also intersects with illness, war, and all of the pain our world is filled with—or how a very real Satan interacts with all of the above? I'm a work in progress on that question. And truth be told, it's a complicated topic necessitating far more than one day's devotional entry. Theologically brilliant men and women have wrestled and continue to wrestle with those questions.[1]

What I do know is that my will (and I've got a strong one) sometimes wants to tell God what to do, or I run ahead of God on my own and then ask him to bless the thing I'm already doing. That's when I set myself up for heartache from unbiblical expectations.

I still pray audaciously, unafraid to ask God for the biggest miracles, but I add what has become an essential second part to my big asks: *Lord, use this situation for your eternal glory, and please allow me to see your fingerprints, your loving presence in the midst of all of it, no matter how you answer my prayers.*

One of my favorite things about God is his loving graciousness toward us as we mature in our faith. I can misunderstand theology even as I am unconditionally loved and used by him. However, our misunderstandings—especially if we do not continue to grow in wisdom and understanding of who God is (and who he is not)—can lead to disastrous consequences, including walking away from God and/or pulling others away from him.

Friends, we are called into spiritual maturity (see 1 Corinthians 3:2; Hebrews 5:14) and into spiritual discernment regarding whether a teaching aligns with Scripture (see 1 John 4:1). This is a never-ending, lifelong journey of growth and nothing to be feared. There is an abiding warmth and intimacy in walking closely with God over a lifetime, especially when we continually seek spiritual wisdom and growth.

Heavenly Father, thank you for grace and patience as we grow in our faith. Nudge us in the areas we are believing wrong theology, that we might gain wisdom, discernment, and nuanced understanding. Amen.

For Reflection:

In what ways have you been mistaken about God over the course of your faith journey? What practices or experiences revealed the truth?

Sacred Rhythms:

Make a plan for continued intellectual spiritual growth, such as joining a Bible study or discussing a theological book with a friend.

There is an abiding warmth and intimacy in walking closely with God over a lifetime, especially when we continually seek spiritual wisdom and growth.

DAY 15

The Power of an Apology

If you are presenting a sacrifice at the altar in the Temple and you suddenly remember that someone has something against you, leave your sacrifice there at the altar. Go and be reconciled to that person. Then come and offer your sacrifice to God.

MATTHEW 5:23-24

"WELL, YOU HAD BETTER GET OVER THAT, KENDRA," my usually soft-spoken mother replied. "Because sometimes you are going to need to hear 'I'm sorry,' and sometimes you are going to need to say it."

I sat back, a little stunned by her strong admonishment.

I had just told her I don't really like apologizing because it's hard and sometimes uncomfortable. Instead of agreeing with me as I expected, she confronted me. Although it wasn't what I wanted to hear then, twenty years later I know she was right to speak so strongly.

Apologies—whether we are giving or receiving them—are a foundational part of any relationship, but especially with those closest to us: our spouse, children, family, and good friends.

I've never found this to be more accurate than with my husband, Kyle. Although we have a good relationship now, we haven't always. We've gone through seasons when one or both of us struggled, and our ability to own our mistakes and apologize has made all the difference.

One thing we've realized is that an "I'm sorry" alone can be empty if it is not followed by a change in our words and actions. I'm as guilty of this as anyone else. I've offered apologies simply as a way to move on without really wanting to change anything about my behavior or words.

This hasn't served me well. Especially in my closest relationships, it set up patterns of behavior that were harder to change as the years went on. But when God showed me how my words and actions were hindering the closeness he meant for me to experience with loved ones, I began attempting to change.

When we remember that someone has something against us, Scripture encourages us to go to them, be reconciled, and then come back to God. He wants us to be in a right relationship with him *and* with others. The two are meant to coexist.

But such a relationship isn't always easy to achieve. It's much easier for me to bring my mistakes or faults to God, asking him to forgive me. It's not always so easy for me to do this with others. To be honest, often I'm afraid of their response. And I may be embarrassed. *How will they view me going forward? Will they even want to forgive me?* Sometimes, I feel shame about what I've said or done, wishing I could go back and change the past.

All these thoughts and more swirl through my brain while I try to conjure up the courage to approach the person I need to apologize to. But the truth is, I always feel better afterward, even if I don't handle the apology perfectly. Even if the other person is still upset, I know I've done what I can do, and some relief comes with trying to make things right.

But when we apologize and then think all the work has been done, it may lead to ongoing trouble. An apology is an excellent place to start, but it's not the end. This is when the work really begins: when we self-assess our words and actions, bring them to God, and ask him for wisdom to do something different going forward. One of the dictionary definitions of repentance is "to feel such sorrow for sin or fault as to be disposed to change one's life for the better."[1]

Compare this definition to what Scripture tells us: "The kind of sorrow God wants us to experience leads us away from sin and results in salvation. There's no regret for that kind of sorrow. But worldly sorrow, which lacks repentance, results in spiritual death" (2 Corinthians 7:10).

To be repentant is to apologize when needed but then to look at ourselves and take action to change for the future. This is the kind of sorrow that leads us away from sin. It's not a worldly sorrow that apologizes in word alone and then moves on, lacking any repentance that would call a person to change. Settling for such surface apologies will lead only to spiritual decline because it will keep us from a life deeply rooted in God. We will also lose the closeness of our relationships with those around us. We'll live an incredibly shallow existence, seeking only those relationships that are comfortable. Such relationships will never sharpen or improve us or build our character.

But there is a maturity that comes when we feel the kind of sorrow God asks of us—the sorrow leading to salvation. We won't regret this kind of sorrow because we know we're working toward a right relationship with God and with those we love. We won't be perfect. God doesn't expect this. Sometimes, we'll stumble. We'll make the same mistakes again. That's okay as long as we keep trying. As a result, we'll see the fruit of our intentions: deeper relationships with God and others.

Which is God's design for us all along.

Lord, thank you for the wisdom that comes from your Word. Please help us to apply it to our lives. If there are apologies we need to make, give us the courage to do so in word and then to follow with our actions and behaviors. May we be people of depth, even when it's hard or uncomfortable. Grow us into maturity in our relationship with you and with those around us. We desire healthy relationships. We love you so much. Thank you for loving us. Amen.

For Reflection:

Is there someone you need to apologize to? Or might any of your words, actions, or behaviors need to change?

Sacred Rhythms:

Apologize to someone today and make a point of ensuring that your words and behaviors back up the apology.

Sometimes, we'll stumble. That's okay as long as we keep trying. We'll see the fruit—deeper relationships with God and others.

DAY 16

The Stories We Tell Ourselves

Who is a God like you, pardoning iniquity and passing over transgression for the remnant of his inheritance? He does not retain his anger forever, because he delights in steadfast love. He will again have compassion on us; he will tread our iniquities underfoot. You will cast all our sins into the depths of the sea.

MICAH 7:18-19, ESV

"I FEEL LEFT OUT, KRISTIN," my friend admitted one day. We were on my porch, curled up on cozy chairs while our kids played upstairs. She looked down at her coffee mug, her voice a little sheepish. "Like I'm back in middle school, feeling bad because I didn't get an invite."

An old high school friend of hers was back in town, and the rest of her friend group had gotten together for dinner—except for my friend, who wasn't invited. She felt sad when she saw photos of them together on social media but wondered if it was childish to feel that way. Was it silly to be hurt by their actions? Even—or especially—if they didn't know how she felt?

"For a while, I thought I had lost touch with the group because we weren't at the same place in life—I was married and had little kids, and they were busy with college and careers. But now, most of them are also married and some have kids, so I don't know what to think," my friend continued. "It feels like they forgot about me."

My friend was doing something most of us have done: writing a story in her mind. She didn't want to feel bitter or resentful, so she was trying to justify the missing invite and give her friends the benefit of the doubt. She had other friends, after all. But the story she was writing in her brain ran something like this: *Maybe we weren't as good of friends as I thought. Maybe their other friendships matter more, or they're better at staying in touch. Or maybe they just don't like who I am now.*

The trouble with writing stories in our minds is that no one can contradict the narrative. If a person doesn't know they hurt our feelings, how can they tell us whether the story we've written is true? Or, if we've created a story in our minds and are using it as a reason to complain about the hurt we feel instead of confronting the person we're mad at, that false story leads us to harbor unforgiveness.

Fred Luskin, founder of the Stanford University Forgiveness Project and author of *Forgive for Good*, says that because our brains are wired to keep us safe from danger, it often exaggerates threats. This means that, often, the story we tell ourselves isn't accurate. We assume the worst-case scenario is correct to protect ourselves.

"We simplify to accentuate the threat. We create these distortions in our head to keep us safe," Luskin explains. He says the fastest way to forgive someone is to rewrite the story we've been telling ourselves.[1]

The truth is that we already have the tools we need because God's grace has rewritten our story. God himself has demonstrated how forgiveness can change the narrative. Micah reminds us that it's because of God's great love for us that he does not hold on to his anger; instead, he has compassion for us. His forgiveness of our sins means that he no longer holds our old narrative against us. And as Christ-followers, we are asked to extend that same mercy to others. Because we are his ambassadors in this world, our actions should reflect his love: "If anyone is in Christ, he is a new creation. The old has passed away; behold, the new has come. All this is from God, who through Christ reconciled us to himself and gave us the ministry of reconciliation" (2 Corinthians 5:17-18, ESV).

Although we are already reconciled to God through his forgiveness of our sins, an integral part of this ministry of reconciliation is doing the work of forgiving others as we have been forgiven. In this sense, rewriting the stories in our minds is something we can do regardless of whether or not other people or our circumstances change.

Forgiveness doesn't mean forgetting, and it doesn't always mean cultivating a relationship with someone who has hurt us—boundaries are essential, especially in toxic relationships and environments. But regardless of the situation, we can rewrite our narrative around it. Even if the other person doesn't want to make changes or remains stuck in an unhealthy pattern, we can focus on getting outside help (from someone like a therapist or a trusted friend), doing internal work to change our own patterns, and rewriting the narrative.

While my friend may never know the reason she didn't receive an invite, she has chosen to rewrite the story in her mind. Instead of holding on to hurt, she tells herself, *No one meant to be unkind. They didn't know I would feel bad or want to be included. They would probably be happy to hear from me if I reached out.* Giving her old friends the benefit of the doubt and choosing to believe the best about them has helped her forgive the hurt they caused, albeit unintentionally.

When we take time to rewrite the stories we tell ourselves, we'll often find that in the same way that grace led to our salvation and rewrote our story, displaying mercy toward others can lead to healing and renewed peace.

Jesus, thank you for rewriting our stories through the power of grace. May we follow your example to rewrite the negative stories in our minds about others, especially friends and family members. Help us to identify stories that may be false in order to find hope and healing through forgiveness. May we seek the tools we need to move forward in health and wholeness. Amen.

For Reflection:

Why do you think we tell ourselves stories that might not be true? What might it mean for us to rewrite the narrative?

Sacred Rhythms:

Jot down a quick list of people who have hurt you that you'd like to forgive. Consider these questions: Does the person know that they hurt my feelings? Is it possible that the story I've told myself isn't accurate? How might I rewrite the story in a way that offers hope and healing?

When we rewrite the stories we tell ourselves, we'll often find that displaying mercy toward others can lead to healing and renewed peace.

DAY 17

Forgiving Ourselves

I will forgive their wickedness, and I will never again remember their sins.

HEBREWS 8:12

"WHAT DO YOU MEAN?" I (Kendra) asked. This person I love dearly had just conveyed to me that he feels depressed and anxious at times over his past and that it still affects his ability to experience joy and peace in the present.

"I just keep thinking about the things I've done," he said, with tears in his eyes.

"But you've asked God to forgive you?" I responded.

"Yes."

"And you know that he *has* forgiven you?"

"Yes."

"And you don't continue in those destructive behaviors?"

"No. I haven't done those things in a long time. Years."

"But you still spend time thinking about them?"

He nodded, his face strained as he stared out the window.

"I guess I don't understand," I said as I struggled to respond in a way that told him I cared. "What good does that do? If you've been forgiven by God and you've changed your ways, why would you still spend time ruminating about the past? You can't change it. What more is there to do?"

He shrugged and shook his head. I felt sad as I watched his internal struggle. He knew what I was saying was true, yet letting go of the pain he has caused others was hard, especially after so many years of holding on to the memories and mistakes.

I prayed with him and thanked him for being honest. I knew it wasn't easy to admit what he was struggling with.

It's almost as if we feel we can pay for our sins by punishing ourselves for them over time. We refuse to let them go, and we allow them to continue bringing us pain. But accepting forgiveness doesn't mean that what we've done doesn't matter or that we aren't acknowledging our wayward ways. It simply means we've recognized our wrongdoing, asked for forgiveness from God and anyone we've hurt, and turned from those ways, determined not to continue the unhealthy behavior.

God's Word assures us that "if we confess our sins to him, he is faithful and just to forgive us our sins and to cleanse us from all wickedness" (1 John 1:9). Confession matters. Acknowledging our sin and the hurt it's caused us and others matters. But once we've worked to make amends, hanging on to our guilt and shame only brings us more pain. It holds us hostage to the past, unable to truly enjoy the present or even dream about the future.

That is not what God wants for any of us.

God wants us healed. Whole. Set free from the things that bound us in the past, whether our own actions or words or those of others. God forgives. It's who he is. And he remembers our wrongdoing no more. He doesn't hold it over our heads, reminding us of how awful we are every time we mess up. He is a good God.

He offers us hope of something better, something new, something that looks more like him. "This means that anyone who belongs to Christ has become a new person. The old life is gone; a new life has begun!" (2 Corinthians 5:17).

The old things are gone. New has come. And with it, an invitation and a purpose.

We have an invitation to follow Christ and to leave old ways behind. And we now have a purpose that involves pursuing love and justice where there had been hate and discord. It involves seeking mercy and kindness where there was unforgiveness and abuse.

But to fulfill this purpose, we must forgive ourselves for our past actions. Sometimes, this means seeking forgiveness from others. Sometimes, it simply means bringing our behavior to God, owning where we've messed up. Then, we are free to walk into the future without fear of a past that no longer has a hold on us and no longer keeps us imprisoned by guilt, shame, or fear.

This new freedom brings forth the possibility of healing.

And we need healing. All of us. It's the only way we'll be able to move on, fulfilling God's purposes for us. God wants us free. Free to experience his love, his peace, his joy. As his Word reminds us, "He has removed our sins as far from us as the east is from the west" (Psalm 103:12).

As far as the east is from the west. That means sin has no more power over us (unless we let it) to keep us entangled in old thoughts, behaviors, and habits. Freedom is ours. This doesn't mean we'll be perfect. We may stumble at times. We are human, and God knows this. That's why his forgiveness is ever-present, ready to meet us and to remind us that there is a better way.

He's not looking for perfection. And neither should we be. All he's looking for is a sincere desire to pursue him first. And when that is our desire, we'll find ourselves looking less and less to old ways that no longer serve us. We'll find we desire new things, godly things. Things that show our love for him and others.

Forgiving ourselves is important. It matters. It's needed.

And if we choose the path of forgiveness, we will walk in freedom, no longer tied to the sins of our past. Secure in the forgiveness God has given us, we can forgive others and, just as importantly, forgive ourselves. We will be able to sow the seeds of love, peace, and joy we've experienced into the world and into the lives of the people around us.

When God says you are forgiven, don't waste any more time holding on to unforgiveness toward yourself.

Lord, thank you for the forgiveness you offer each of us. Show us where we have lived contrary to your ways. Open our eyes so we aren't blind to our sin. Help us to pursue forgiveness from others, if necessary, and from you. And once we've done all we can, show us how to forgive ourselves. Remove the guilt and shame we are feeling. Help us walk each day in the freedom of your forgiveness. We are so grateful for the mercy you extended to us. Your compassion that is freely given to each one of us. Your unending love. May we always run to you first when we mess up. We love you so much. Amen.

For Reflection:

In what area of your life have you struggled to walk in the freedom of forgiving yourself?

Sacred Rhythms:

Bring your unforgiveness of yourself to God and ask him to show you how to release your past mistakes to him and move forward on a new path.

We may stumble at times. We are human, and God knows this. That's why his forgiveness is ever-present, ready to meet us and to remind us that there is a better way.

DAY 18

For Further Reflection

1. What stood out to you about forgiveness this week? What surprised or inspired you? What tested or challenged you?

2. What insights did you gain through this week's fast from comfort and convenience so you could put the needs of others first or put yourself in someone else's shoes?

3. How do you forgive well, and where can you work to improve?

Lord, thank you for modeling what forgiveness looks like through your atoning death on the cross. Thank you for bridging the separation created by sin to bring us back to our heavenly Father, that we might have access to the throne room. Show us who we need to forgive, regardless of how the other person responds or whether they ever even know. Walk alongside us in situations where forgiveness feels hard, reminding us that we are not in this alone. Give us the boldness and bravery to apologize, assume responsibility for hurt we've caused, and seek our own forgiveness. And Lord, help us to forgive ourselves. Amen.

WEEK 4

PEACE AND CONTENTMENT

Sunday–Saturday

DAY 19

Peace in the Tension of Life

Come to me, all of you who are weary and carry heavy burdens, and I will give you rest. Take my yoke upon you. Let me teach you, because I am humble and gentle at heart, and you will find rest for your souls. For my yoke is easy to bear, and the burden I give you is light.

MATTHEW 11:28-30

"IS THIS REALLY ALL YOU WANT, KENDRA?" Kyle asked one night as we were tidying up the house.

"What do you mean?" I asked, picking up the stuffed animals that'd been forgotten about after dinner. Our young family was settled in bed for the night, and I was tired. I am not usually a night person, so my husband's question left me strained. "What more do *you* want?"

Seeing my frustration, he paused. "Sorry," he said. "I don't mean to stress you out."

"I want you to explain more, but can we please not do it right now?" I asked. "Let's talk in the morning."

Kyle nodded as he continued to help me pick up.

It's a familiar conversation, one we've had several times over our twenty-plus years of marriage. Kyle has many gifts, but there is one that I thought of as a curse for a long time: his often unsettled feelings about wanting to be sure that we and our family are not stagnant in our faith. Although these feelings have sometimes caused strain, they have pushed our family outside of our daily habits to love other people as God has told us to.

If I'm honest, I've needed this prompting. I am a creature of habit, and I like my daily routines. There's nothing wrong with that—it has created a lot of stability within our family—but the downside is that I can become stuck and rigid. I am sometimes less than willing to rearrange our family patterns, allow for change, or grow in ways God would call us to.

I've learned to be sensitive to my husband's rumblings, knowing that we balance one another. I've also learned to appreciate the tension of juggling between my need for consistency and schedule, and the need to allow for disruptions from God that are ultimately good for our family. I have found that there can be peace in the tension.

And that's important. There is no greater frustration than feeling like you've gotten everything that should bring contentment, yet having it remain elusive. Even when everything is as I think it should be, peace does not always follow.

Many times, we look for peace and contentment in the wrong places. We think it can be found in the perfect job, house, relationship, environment, social group . . . And yet. Even when we finally attain those things, we find peace and contentment lacking or fleeting.

So where *do* we find peace, no matter what is happening?

We find it by coming to Jesus. By laying down our burdens—all the things we're striving to be and do and accomplish—and leaning into his promise to give us rest and peace for our souls. The burden he gives us is light.

So many of the things we pursue aren't things he would ask of us. It's not that they are necessarily bad or wrong. They're just not the most important things.

This week, we want to come to Jesus, lay down our burdens, and find peace and contentment. Whether we are in a season of rest or busyness, Jesus' promise is for each of us. He meets us where we are and whispers, "Lay down your burdens and find rest. Take my yoke. It's light."

Lean into his promise.

This Week's Fasting Focus

This week, we want to bring peace to our lives and hearts by practically decluttering our homes, workspaces, or any other environment within our care. It doesn't have to be a complete overhaul. It's okay to start small. Is there a nagging closet you haven't organized or cleaned out yet? Or maybe just the pile of mail in the corner of the kitchen?

Next, we want to look at our calendars. How are you spending your time? Is the use of your days intentional, or are you flowing along with life? Are there activities you can remove from your schedule? Or maybe you need to add something that brings more peace, such as a dinner out with a friend.

We know this can feel like a lot, but please don't be overwhelmed. There is no expectation to accomplish more. This exercise is simply meant to help you become more aware of ways to bring peace instead of strife into your life by being sensitive to God and listening for his direction.

Lord, thank you for the comfort you offer us. Thank you for providing us with rest and peace. Give us wisdom as we seek you and look to take on the yoke you would have for us, while laying down burdens you never asked us to carry. We love you, Jesus. Thank you for journeying with us through life. Amen.

DAY 20

Embracing Peace as We Wait on God

Blessed are those who trust in the LORD and have made the LORD their hope and confidence. They are like trees planted along a riverbank, with roots that reach deep into the water. Such trees are not bothered by the heat or worried by long months of drought. Their leaves stay green, and they never stop producing fruit.

JEREMIAH 17:7-8

AS A YOUNGER VERSION OF JULIE slipped behind the wheel of an older model Toyota, I was tired but happy. My bridesmaid duties complete, I let my mind wander down memory lane as the car ate up miles of pavement through the prairies of western Minnesota. Fond reminiscences of college high jinks with the bride and groom slowly turned to thoughts of the cute groomsman "randomly" assigned to escort me down the aisle and my friends' attempts to set us up.

I silently berated myself for being, once again, too shy to vie for a young man's attention among the other single ladies. Regret shifted to planning, and I considered how I might finagle a second contact with him since we both lived in the Twin Cities. As my head whirled with possibilities, I paused as an extra loud thought passed through my mind: *Perhaps you ought to pray about reaching out to him.*

Agreeing with that loud thought, I sent up a simple, flippant prayer: *Dear Jesus, should I contact that handsome groomsman?* Prayer complete, I turned my mind to graduate school obligations and the long drive ahead as I flipped on the radio.

A popular country song immediately filled the car with lyrics about rearview mirrors and driving away from a cute guy with nary a glance backward.

I paused, flicking my eyes to the rearview mirror and the memory of the groomsman I was rapidly leaving behind. I snapped off the radio and prayed again, this time with focus: *Lord, I have no idea if you were speaking to me through that song or not, but I'm not going to contact him. Either he can connect with me or not; I'm going to trust you.*

What I didn't know, couldn't know, was that a fellow student named Aaron—funny, handsome, extroverted, and sweet—was, only two weeks into the future, going to ask me to go for a walk. And because I wouldn't be involved with anyone else, my shy younger self was going to say yes, kicking off a love story that has endured for more than two decades.

But God knew. And God knew that I would have turned down that walk with Aaron if I had set up a date with that groomsman.

Had I not listened to the still, small voice on that lonely drive home, would I have dated and married Aaron? I don't know. I do know that, had I not listened to that quiet voice, at best, I would have met my husband only after unnecessary complications and, perhaps, after serious heartache.

That early lesson has become our family's mantra: It is far better to wait within God's will and his timing than to run ahead of him. Is it easy? No. But I'm learning to lean into waiting seasons, embracing Psalm 37:7, rather than impatiently trying to hurry God along: "Be still in the presence of the Lord, and wait patiently for him to act. Don't worry about evil people who prosper or fret about their wicked schemes."

Unsurprisingly, many of my waiting seasons have been full of silver linings, despite my sometimes-grumpy heart. I have a coworker-turned-best-friend whom I met only because she started at the same company while I was still there, anxiously awaiting my next adventure. As we impatiently waited for Aaron's first job offer post-graduation, we received another precious gift: That waiting season allowed Aaron to spend time with his ill father. These are but two small additional examples of times we have, in retrospect, repeatedly thanked God for the gift found in delayed answers to prayers.

I've also realized that waiting seasons (or difficult experiences) develop my character. I am admittedly a work in progress spiritually, emotionally, and experientially, and sometimes there is a forced pause for me to grow into a role before the next door (or window) opens. The apostle Paul captures this progression perfectly:

> We can rejoice, too, when we run into problems and trials, for we know that they help us develop endurance. And endurance develops strength of character, and character strengthens our confident hope of salvation. And this hope will not lead to disappointment. For we know how dearly God loves us, because he has given us the Holy Spirit to fill our hearts with his love.
>
> ROMANS 5:3-5

As little as I like them and as much as they sometimes baffle me, I've learned that waiting seasons are valuable to my growth as a follower of Jesus and are opportunities to get about his work in powerful ways. God does not abandon us in our waiting seasons, and we can choose peace and strength in trusting his will and his timing. As his Word promises, "Those who trust in the LORD will find new strength. They will soar high on wings like eagles. They will run and not grow weary. They will walk and not faint" (Isaiah 40:31).

When I wait, I pray for discernment and wisdom—asking God what divine appointments he might have for me in this way station of life and what important lessons I might learn while I'm here. That change in perspective helps me embrace peace and even contentment rather than desperately trying to push my way into a different circumstance.

Heavenly Father, reframe our perspective in seasons of waiting. Show us silver linings possible only because of our waiting. Reveal what you have for us to do, both externally as we serve as the hands and feet of Christ and internally as we continue to develop spiritual maturity. Give us peace, and help us cultivate contentment even as you hear our prayers and move on our behalf behind the scenes. Amen.

For Reflection:

Reconsider a time when you were waiting for God to move. What silver linings do you see in retrospect? How did God use you to impact others? How did your faith mature?

Sacred Rhythms:

How will you intentionally embrace peace in current or future waiting seasons?

Waiting seasons are valuable to our growth as followers of Jesus. God does not abandon us, and we can choose peace and strength in trusting his will and his timing.

DAY 21

Going Smaller

Beware! Guard against every kind of greed.
Life is not measured by how much you own.

LUKE 12:15

IT WAS SEVERAL YEARS AGO that we first got the bug to move out of our home. We'd lived there for seven years, and our kids were getting older. It seemed the right time to find something else, something larger and more spacious.

"Isn't this the obvious next step in our life?" I (Kendra) asked my husband, Kyle. He agreed with me.

We talked with our mortgage broker, who gave us an amount we could afford for a new, upgraded house, and we started looking.

A few days later, we found what we thought was the house of our dreams. It had everything we wanted, down to the paint color. Nothing would need to be fixed or remodeled. Over the next several days, I began to imagine us in the house, in our kids' rooms, and in the big backyard.

But just as quickly as we'd found it, it was gone. The market was moving fast, and another buyer secured a contract before we could.

I was frustrated but determined to find something else. I continued to look throughout our area for possible homes on the outskirts of town, preferably with some land. We viewed several more, but there was always something Kyle didn't like about the house. I started to feel like he was being too picky.

"Nothing's going to be perfect," I told him, but he still felt very strongly about finding just what we were looking for.

As the weeks and months went by with little movement on our part, God began working in our hearts. We felt him wanting us to move closer to the heart of our city, not away from it.

Not knowing we were both starting to have the same nudge, we sat down one evening to discuss the potential move.

"I feel like God may be asking us to go smaller, not bigger," I said, unsure how my husband would respond.

"Me too," he agreed.

"Really?"

"Yeah."

"Maybe that's why you haven't liked anything so far," I teased.

"Maybe," he said with a grin.

As we talked about what we now knew God was laying on both our hearts, we got out our computer and began a new search for homes—ones that were less expensive and closer to the center of our city. We found several we wanted to walk through, then called Kyle's sister, April, and our brother-in-law, Rob, who were also our realtors. We explained to them what we were thinking. Being Christians, they understood and were excited about where God was leading us.

The following week, they showed us several homes. We loved one of them, but it would need a lot of work. As we prepared an offer, Rob told us that several more had just come in.

"Maybe that's not it," Kyle said, and we continued to look.

Not long after, we found another house we were excited about from the pictures. We hoped the reality was as lovely as what we saw online.

As we walked into the front porch area, my usually picky husband said, "This is it."

Rob and I both looked at him, surprised, and laughed.

"Really?" I asked. "Do you want to see the rest of the house?"

"Sure. But this is it," he responded.

As Rob walked us through the rest of the house, it became clear that it was the right one. It felt like the place we were meant to move to next.

"He's right," I said to Rob. "This is it."

We made an offer and quickly heard that it had been accepted.

As we packed our belongings and the moving day approached, some loved ones questioned why we would make such a move. "Are you having money issues?" "Why would you buy an older, less expensive house?" "Is the neighborhood safe?"

We assured everyone we were fine, explaining that we felt God was leading us to this new home. The first week after we moved in, I slept better than I had in years. We had peace about this new space and the new neighborhood, and especially about listening to God's leading even if others didn't fully understand.

We still have that peace. I love this house, and it fits our family. Since it was less expensive than our previous home, we've been able to pay off the smaller mortgage more quickly. This gives us more flexibility to be generous and to weather the financial ebbs and flows of owning our own business, since we aren't weighed down by debt. We're not perfect—we've made our share of financial mistakes—but going smaller instead of bigger is one of the smartest things we've ever done.

Our culture will often tell us the path to success: Buy up and more when you can. Bigger houses. Nicer vehicles. More stuff. Although there's certainly nothing wrong with nice things, they can become a problem when we think they will bring us contentment. Peace of mind and heart aren't waiting to be found just around the corner once we've reached the next level of success (or stuff).

Peace isn't found in a big house any more than it is in a small one. It's a lie to think, *I'll finally be happy when I have (fill in the blank).* It's simply not true. Or if that object does bring us happiness for a time, it'll be fleeting. Soon enough, we'll find ourselves longing for the next thing that we think will bring us contentment.

The good news is, we can have peace today. We can find contentment in what we already have when we start recognizing all that is ours in Christ and when we see the goodness around us, however small it might be.

There's a reason Jesus said our life isn't to be measured by how much we own. That's not where we find our worth or our peace. He goes on in Luke 12:21 to say that it's foolish to store up earthly wealth but not have a rich relationship with God. That is what truly matters. And that is where we'll find peace that won't fade, fall apart, wear out, or break down.

Lord, thank you for making contentment and peace attainable today. Help us not to look to material things to fill what only you can. Let us be content with what we have already been given, and even as we gain more, help us never to look to those things to satisfy us in place of you. We love you, Jesus. Amen.

For Reflection:

In what things have you tried to find contentment only to be disappointed once you attained them? How is God teaching you contentment in your current season?

Sacred Rhythms:

Go through your house with a box and gather items you no longer need or want. Find a place to donate them.

The good news is, we can have peace today. We can find contentment when we start recognizing all that is ours in Christ.

DAY 22

Calendar Clutter

This is the day the L*ORD has made. We will rejoice and be glad in it.*

PSALM 118:24

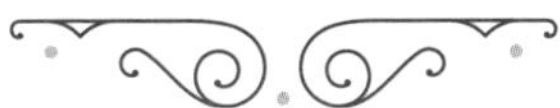

"HOW ARE YOU?" I asked a friend as we walked side by side out of church. The service had just ended, and I'd warmly said hello when I met her in the aisle.

"Good, Kristin," she said reflexively, then paused. "Busy."

With that, she launched into a laundry list of the many sports her children were in, the committee she had joined in a leadership role, and the coaching her husband had agreed to. Finished recounting the many commitments on her family's proverbial plate, she laughingly lamented how she and her husband hardly saw each other in the evenings because they were so busy driving from one activity to the next.

I nodded along, understanding.

Life is busy. It's a common refrain. But is this constant state of motion necessary? Why do we wear busyness like a coveted badge of honor?

On the one hand, being busy helps us feel valued and validated. Perhaps we say yes to new responsibilities because we feel like we should. Maybe we say yes because we admire the person asking or don't want to disappoint them. We say yes because it's nice to feel needed or wanted or simply because it's the path of least resistance.

But the truth is that every yes we give is a no to something else, and the unintended consequences can be far-reaching. Relationships lag because we're too busy to give someone our full, undistracted attention or the time necessary for a deep, authentic connection. Or we skim the surface of our lives, offering busyness as a convenient excuse as to why we haven't responded to an email, made time for exercise, or had a difficult conversation.

Calendar clutter necessitates mental clutter too. This leaves little margin for rest, healthy rhythms, or the ability to think creatively or critically. Instead, we rush from one place to the next, ignoring the finite nature of our time, resources, and energy. You and I were not meant to race from pillar to post, running ourselves ragged to measure up. Filling our calendar in our search for significance will only make us tired, defeated, and overwhelmed. Even though we know that "this is the day the Lord has made" (Psalm 118:24), we are often unimpressed by the truth that today is a gift unlike any other, never to be repeated.

Yet our significance isn't found in what we do or don't do on any given day; it's in our identity as God's beloved children. That identity isn't contingent on how much or how little we accomplish. Did we overlook or forgive a minor slight, a late appointment, or our child's unkind tone? Did we thank someone for their work or how they made someone else feel? Did we love our neighbor today? All those are measures of "success" too.

As we focus on decluttering our home of unnecessary items this week, perhaps it's time to consider our schedule as well. Maybe it's time to reconsider what's taking up room in our hearts and minds, spilling over into our calendars and overtaking our lives.

What does mental decluttering look like? When it comes to our calendar, it could be a simple math issue—too many things on the list. Or maybe it's a deeper decluttering we need: removing expectations of who we are or what we want to be by deleting podcasts we don't listen to, music we don't enjoy, books we "should" read but never do, emails that bog us down, subscriptions we aren't using, or social media apps that drain us.

Perhaps the true mental clutter is less obvious: the silent clutter of comparison or perfectionism. The unspoken judgment of other people's opinions, or the feeling that we haven't met goals or achievements we once aspired to. The weight of guilt, the past, or fractured relationships. While we can't see that clutter, it wears on our hearts.

I love how *The Message* talks about living your life without comparing it to anyone else's:

> Make a careful exploration of who you are and the work you have been given, and then sink yourself into that. Don't be impressed with yourself. Don't compare yourself with others. Each of you must take responsibility for doing the creative best you can with your own life.
>
> GALATIANS 6:4-5

What does our creative best look like? And how does that impact the way our calendar looks? Let's consider dividing our time rather than our attention by setting boundaries for tasks. And when we consider saying yes, let's ask a few questions:

- If I say yes to this request, what else am I saying yes to? (Additional tasks on top of current workload, responsibility to others, periodic meetings, spending money on necessary items?)
- Does the additional cost or workload warrant that yes? (Being part of something bigger than what you could do on your own, finding purpose, helping others, being active in the community, demonstrating God's love, collaborating?)
- What am I saying no to? (Time with family, an hour or two to relax in the evening?)

Answering these questions will provide a framework for approaching our schedule.

In the summer, our family completes a Summer Bucket List that includes ice cream for dinner, a backyard treasure hunt, science projects, mini golfing, and visiting the children's museum.

But we also have many ordinary days when we don't do anything on the list.

"I want to do something special," my children complain. A day at home feels insignificant, if not wasteful of summer's beauty and brevity.

Unluckily for them, while I love our bucket list, I don't want to have something on my calendar every day. Blank spaces are something to be celebrated, not sighed over—an endless expanse of possibility, not a reason to feel dismayed. A few years ago, I heard that instead of "FOMO" (fear of missing out), people were talking about "JOMO" (joy of missing out). The idea resonated with me. When we create margin in our lives—when we leave blank slots in our calendar—we create spaces with infinite possibility and creativity. We have time to laugh, to breathe, to dream. We make room for God to move and for us to notice him at work in our lives. We open ourselves to new opportunities or permit ourselves to rest, finding peace on the other side.

Jesus, thank you that we are not judged by how much we accomplish in a day. Your grace is all we need, today and every day. Help us to appreciate today for the gift that it is. Amen.

For Reflection:

Does your calendar reflect the things that matter to you? If not, how could you make space for rest, creativity, or other priorities? What would it look like for you to "schedule" rest?

Sacred Rhythms:

Identify at least two things you can declutter from your calendar today.

When we create margin in our lives, we create spaces with infinite possibility. We have time to laugh, to breathe, to dream. We make room for God to move.

DAY 23

All That We Need

The LORD *is my shepherd; I have all that I need.*

PSALM 23:1

ONCE A YEAR, I (KRISTIN) TEXT A FRIEND OF MINE and ask if she wants to do another gratitude accountability challenge with me. The idea is simple: Once a day, I text my friend three things I am grateful for, and she responds with her three things. The challenge lasts two weeks, but studies have shown that participating in this kind of challenge can boost your mood for up to six months afterward.[1]

Though I'm grateful for the "big stuff"—family, friends, faith, home, food—I'm always surprised at how much more specific my daily list is and how often it includes items on a much smaller scale. Scrolling back through my texts after the challenge, I realize how grateful I am for small comforts like hot coffee, the sun streaming through my windows, and books piled up in my living room. It's often those little things—a cardinal flitting through my backyard, a heartfelt late-night conversation with my daughter, or a cloudless sky on my way to school drop-off—that I appreciate most.

Given how detailed the natural world is and the level of care our Creator has invested in it, it shouldn't be surprising that God concerns himself with the big picture as well as the minutiae of the earth and everyone in it. It also should come as no surprise that Jesus, who taught us how to pray and demonstrated how to live, offered an example of how to give thanks for the small things.

In Mark 6, we find the story of Jesus teaching a large crowd in a remote place. As it grew late, his disciples suggested that he send the people to the surrounding countryside and villages to get something to eat. Jesus responded that the disciples should feed them, but when they went looking for food among the people, they discovered the vastly insufficient amount of five loaves of bread and two fish.

But Jesus took the loaves and fish, looked to heaven, and gave thanks. He then broke the food in pieces and directed the disciples to feed the crowds. Miraculously, the disciples collected twelve baskets of leftovers. Jesus had turned five loaves of bread and two fish into enough food for more than five thousand people, with plenty to spare.

It's noteworthy that when Jesus prayed, he gave thanks for the little things—the "boring" things, even. Though I love bread in all its many forms, and certain types of non-fishy fish are enjoyable to me, I'm still struck by the idea that he gave thanks for such mundane items. Because on days when I'm folding a seemingly bottomless pile of clean clothes, plunging my hands into hot, soapy water to scrub dishes, or adding tiny chocolate chips to my daughter's favorite pancake batter, I take comfort in knowing that these small efforts matter too. If Jesus gave thanks for a simple meal of two items—no gourmet, four-course feast here—then so can I.

The other thing to appreciate about Jesus' prayer for the fish and loaves is that he thanked God *before* the miracle occurred. He didn't wait until after his disciples had distributed the food or cleaned up the leftovers.

Much of life happens in those in-between, not-yet moments. You and I can take comfort in knowing that Jesus understands what it means to wait and to give thanks even as we wait. Even before the miracle occurs. (Even if, in our imperfect world, it never occurs this side of heaven.) Because oftentimes, we can be so focused on waiting for the big things to happen—for our loved one to be healed, our dream job to appear, the perfect house to come on the market—that we forget to notice and appreciate the little things.

Yet peace and contentment don't come from achieving or acquiring those big things but from noticing and appreciating small, daily reasons to be grateful. Food on the table. Clothes on our backs. Life itself. Fish and bread.

As a child, I learned the version of Psalm 23:1 that says, "The Lord is my shepherd; I shall not want" (NKJV). Though I could recite the whole psalm, my young brain glossed over that first verse to get to what I saw as the "good stuff," like the Lord walking with me through the valley of the shadow of death and preparing a table before me in the presence of my enemies. Those parts of the psalm felt more dramatic and exciting.

But as an adult, I find the first verse compelling enough to stop and ponder it. While as a child it didn't seem likely that I would ever "not want," I've since realized that alternate translations include "I have all that I need" (NLT) and "I lack nothing" (NIV). This phrase resonates on a deeper level now. When we hold fast to the truth that with Jesus we already have all we need and we lack nothing, our view shifts from scarcity to abundance. If we can see our lives as lacking nothing, we'll be better able to recognize the blessings that should inspire gratitude in us each day. Then, peace and contentment will be ours for the asking.

Jesus, thank you for demonstrating gratitude in your life and ministry. Help us do the same by recognizing reasons to be grateful—big and small—in our daily lives. May we foster contentment by seeing that we already have all that we need in you. Amen.

For Reflection:

In what ways does the phrase "I have all that I need" help us to shift our mindset from scarcity to abundance? How can practicing gratitude help us cultivate peace and contentment?

Sacred Rhythms:

List three things you're grateful for today. (Bonus: Ask a friend to do a two-week gratitude challenge with you.)

Peace and contentment don't come from achieving or acquiring big things but from noticing and appreciating small, daily reasons to be grateful.

DAY 24

Choosing Joy

I pray that God, the source of hope, will fill you completely with joy and peace because you trust in him. Then you will overflow with confident hope through the power of the Holy Spirit.

ROMANS 15:13

"CONGRATULATIONS! THIS REQUIRES A CELEBRATION with my secret stash of the 'Really Good Chocolate'!" My emailed response was to one of my advisees, a student I'd been walking alongside for several semesters in my role at a local college.

When my student came (literally) dancing through my office door an hour later, she was laughing. "Julie, can you believe that I got into the grad school I wanted?! I'm so excited, relieved, and just SO EXCITED!"

If humans had tails, hers would have been wagging. And her energy was contagious. As I pulled my Lindor Truffles and Ghirardelli Chocolate Squares from their secret hiding place, I was grinning. "This definitely calls for the really good stuff. Now, tell me all about it."

And she did. We enjoyed a bite of something decadent as she gave me all the details of her early admission, of where she was thinking of living, of what she hoped to do post–grad school. She and I paused our days to revel in her accomplishment, and the time spent was a highlight of my week.

I didn't always respond to special moments this way. In fact, I skipped over so many milestones in my early life, certain that I hadn't accomplished anything worthy of celebrating. Instead, I'd cast my eyes upon the next goal and plunge forward, back to work toward the next milestone, promising myself I'd celebrate when I'd truly "arrived."

The sad thing about that lifestyle is that you never *do* arrive. There is always something next to strive for. And someone else is always doing the same thing you've done, only bigger and better. You can't possibly celebrate when you aren't officially at the top of the heap.

Oh friend, what a miserable, discontented way to live! We are always striving, consumed with the future rather than the present, and yet that's often the way we are encouraged to live. I've started calling it "aspirational living"—I've been so focused on future goals and plans that I've forgotten to find myself and others fully alive in the present moment.

But now? With my hope and trust placed firmly in Jesus, I make plans for the future, but I am not consumed by those plans, nor am I worried about what tomorrow holds. And with that firm foundation of hope and trust, I find peace and joy in today. I hunt for reasons to celebrate God's goodness, to savor joy, to exclaim excitedly over anything delightful and good and lovely.

I will gladly be *that* unsophisticated woman who gawks awkwardly with a tug on Aaron's arm to halt—even if it impedes the flow of pedestrian traffic—to fully take in beautiful art, gorgeous architecture, or an unbroken shell on the beach. I do not—and will not—play it cool and glamorous and like I've seen it all before. I will bury my nose ridiculously deep in a lilac hedge during an evening walk, wade through the frigid waters of Lake Superior to fish out a rock that might be an agate, or spam my friends' inboxes with texts and too many emojis when I'm proud of whatever hard thing they have accomplished.

What changed? I finally realized that joy—a fruit of the Spirit (see Galatians 5:22)—is evidence of the Holy Spirit at work in our lives; it is external evidence of our internal faith. But what surprised me, at least at first, was how closely Scripture ties joy to peace.

Today's verse tells us that joy and peace come from placing our trust and hope in God. And Romans 14:17-18 reminds us that God's Kingdom is concerned with "living a life of goodness and peace and joy in the Holy Spirit."

Choosing joy does not mean we ignore hard situations. It means we entrust God with the hard and the good. We can find joy, choose joy, even as we deeply grieve.

What does it look like to choose joy? I've discovered that the more intentional I am about choosing joy, the easier it is to spot.

One way I find joy is in marveling at God's creation. It helps to spend time around toddlers or someone new to an experience (or at least to consider what something would look like through that lens). There is so much about the world that we grow accustomed to and allow to fade into the background unless we practice noticing.

I was on a flight about three years ago when an early elementary–age child exclaimed loudly from the window seat across the aisle, "Mom! We're in heaven; look at the sun shining on top of the clouds!"

Several of us in the vicinity chuckled as window shades went up so people could take in the view from that child's perspective. It is much the same with tourists and locals—you can always tell who the tourists are because we're the ones gaping at whatever is lovely or intriguing or bizarre as the locals zip around us.

I also find joy in celebrating good news and accomplishments, big and small, whether my own or someone else's. I keep "regular" chocolate in a bowl on my office desk, available to all and stocked all year round. That stash of "really good" chocolate stays out of sight, produced with a flourish to make whomever I share it with feel special and loved. It's a big deal to be offered the "good" chocolate, and I want to keep it that way. My husband and I often celebrate milestones with a dinner date or take-out. We've surprised friends with cake and flowers for a big anniversary. I've dropped into a friend's workplace with a favorite coffee order. Texts, funny cards in the mail—the ways and opportunities to celebrate someone are as endless as your creativity!

Every time I choose joy, I am reminded of God's goodness. And that reminder is almost always followed by peace—just as Scripture tells us.

Heavenly Father, help us to see joy not as frivolous and silly but as an outward expression of our internal trust and hope in you. As we practice choosing joy, give us peace—over our tomorrows, over our situation, over our loved ones. Amen.

For Reflection:

Consider all the things that bring you joy, and then consider the things that bring joy to those you love.

Sacred Rhythms:

Do something joy-filled for yourself today, and do something joy-filled for someone around you this week.

Choosing joy does not mean we ignore hard situations. It means we entrust God with the hard and the good. We can find joy, choose joy, even as we deeply grieve.

DAY 25

For Further Reflection

1. What stood out to you about peace and contentment this week? What surprised or inspired you? What tested or challenged you?

2. What insights did you gain through this week's fast of decluttering your home and your calendar?

3. How do you live out peace and contentment well, and where can you work to improve?

____

____

____

____

Heavenly Father, thank you for the peace and contentment you offer each of us. As we reflect over this past week, open our eyes to things we've clung to that don't offer lasting peace. May we instead embrace the things that matter most while leaning into the joy you give freely. We love you. Continue to help us loosen our grasp on things that can't offer lasting peace, and may we turn to you first in all things. We are forever grateful for your grace. Amen.

WEEK 5

GENEROSITY

Sunday–Saturday

DAY 26

The Ultimate Generosity

This is how God loved the world: He gave his one and only Son, so that everyone who believes in him will not perish but have eternal life. God sent his Son into the world not to judge the world, but to save the world through him.

JOHN 3:16-17

IT WAS AN ULTRA-EARLY MONDAY MORNING as I turned down a local gym's hallway toward the Pilates studio, back after a multiple-year hiatus. Feeling excited to be back and slightly sheepish for my too-long time away, I heard my instructor's voice from just outside the studio door even before I saw her: "Julie, YOU'RE BACK! I was so excited to see your name on the registration sheet for this morning!"

The warmth in her tone set me at ease as I followed her into the studio. "Mary, have you met Julie? She was part of the six a.m. crew a while back, and maybe you guys were in the same class together. She's come back to us!"

Women smiled warmly at me as they stretched, settling into position before class began. As I settled into position myself, I couldn't help but send a silent thank-you heavenward. While I hadn't expected anyone to be mean, I hadn't anticipated the warmth and immediate acceptance back into this tiny community of Pilates early birds. No one asked why I'd been away. There was no shame as I relearned some of the movements. And it wasn't five minutes before someone cracked a joke and we were all laughing even as our muscles quivered from a particularly intense set of exercises. It felt good to be back and a bit like I'd never left at all, emotionally at least.

As I walked toward my car after that first session, I couldn't help but think of the prodigal son—not because my extended absence from an exercise class was a sin, but because of the exuberant and generous welcome I received upon my return.

In the story, as you may recall, the younger of two sons demands his inheritance early and, being granted it, leaves home for a distant land, squandering his legacy on "wild living" (Luke 15:12-13). Destitute as a famine sweeps the land, the son eventually returns home filled with shame, prepared to beg his father to let him be a servant and at least have food and lodging, knowing he no longer deserves to be a son.

> So he returned home to his father. And while he was still a long way off, his father saw him coming. Filled with love and compassion, he ran to his son, embraced him, and kissed him. His son said to him, "Father, I have sinned against both heaven and you, and I am no longer worthy of being called your son."
>
> But his father said to the servants, "Quick! Bring the finest robe in the house and put it on him. Get a ring for his finger and

> sandals for his feet. And kill the calf we have been fattening. We must celebrate with a feast, for this son of mine was dead and has now returned to life. He was lost, but now he is found." So the party began.
>
> LUKE 15:20-24

When I put myself in the position of that lost son (and haven't most of us been at various levels of rebellion toward God at some point about something?), I can't help but get misty-eyed at the unmerited, loving generosity of the father's warm welcome. While there certainly would be a conversation later with consequences laid out, that welcome back into an intimate relationship was exactly what the son needed as he trudged down the road toward home.

The prodigal's father represents God and his reaction when we return to him through repentance and forgiveness, and God's actions match his parable: He sent his only beloved Son to (voluntarily) die for our sins, that we might have a way back into intimate relationship with him through Jesus (see John 3:16-17). Is there anything more generous than that intentional sacrifice? Of course, God's generosity toward us goes beyond salvation in a myriad of ways, but that's where it starts.

As followers of Jesus, we are called to lives of generosity. The New Testament is replete with exhortations and examples of what generosity looks like, with our material possessions (see Matthew 6:21; Acts 20:35; 2 Corinthians 9:7, 11-12; Galatians 6:2; 1 Timothy 6:17-19; 1 John 3:17) but also with our prayer, forgiveness, love, and hospitality for one another (see Mathew 5:44; 18:21-22; John 13:34; Hebrews 13:2).

This Week's Fasting Focus

This week, we are practicing generosity—physically, emotionally, and spiritually. With respect to the physical, we are embracing a "no unnecessary spending" week. That might mean that we'll buy milk but eat meals primarily from what we already have in the pantry and freezer. And what we save from forgoing that coffee treat or the swing by the thrift store over lunch (or whatever unnecessary purchases we indulge in) will be the start of our own "blessing budget," or family giving fund (see Day 29), to be gifted to an individual, family, or organization in prayerful partnership with God.

Our spiritual and emotional generosity will be inspired (and perhaps stretched) by our daily prompts this week. The goal is to embrace generosity (physical, emotional, and spiritual) as a foundational part of our faithful walk alongside Jesus.

Heavenly Father, thank you for the ultimate gift of Jesus' life—both for his earthly example of how we are to pattern our lives and for his death and resurrection that brings us back into right standing with you. Help us reexamine generosity through Scripture, prayer, and actions—correcting any mistaken notions we might have while also showing us how powerfully generosity without strings reveals your love for the world. Help us go on an adventure of generosity with you this week, and in that process forever change our hearts and the lives of others around us. Amen.

DAY 27

No-Strings Generosity

Tell them to use their money to do good. They should be rich in good works and generous to those in need, always being ready to share with others. By doing this they will be storing up their treasure as a good foundation for the future so that they may experience true life.

1 TIMOTHY 6:18-19

"THE GOOD NEWS IS THAT we received an extremely generous donation from a local foundation," reported the financial guru of a nonprofit board my (Julie's) friend serves on.

The board chair waited a beat before responding, "That's the news we've been hoping for! And the bad news? Is there bad news? How can this be bad news?"

"Well . . ."

A different board member spoke up, "It's a restricted gift. We can only use it for a very specific set of conditions."

"And those conditions are . . . ?" the board chair began before being interrupted by the newest board member's exclamation: "You mean we can't use it to fix the roof? That's—by far—our most urgent need!"

By now, the entire board of directors was leaning forward, their focus intent upon the finance director's reply. "Um. No. We can't use it for the roof. The donors were clear that it must be used for programming, not for capital improvements . . ."

A chorus of groans echoed throughout the room as grateful but frustrated board members absorbed the news. The funding would be put to good use, but how to fix the most immediate need remained a worrisome concern.

Almost every nonprofit board has encountered this struggle between gratitude and regret over restricted gifts. While they are delighted to have funding and investment, sometimes the strings attached to generosity are so limiting and onerous that they reduce the value and usability of the gift.

Listening to my friend's recounting of the board meeting and her request for continued prayer for a new roof, I recognized both sides of the situation. The donors—wanting to be good stewards and see their money put to good use—placed restrictions on how the money could be spent. The nonprofit—knowing their most urgent concern—needed flexibility and trust that the donated resources would be used effectively and efficiently. The donors were well-intentioned, but their restrictions added complexity rather than easing a burden.

As I washed dishes the next afternoon, my thoughts returned to my friend's small but mighty nonprofit and that gift of currently unusable money. *Lord, do I do that? Do I attach strings to my generosity in ways you don't require? Ways that cause damage or harm, even temporarily?*

The answer is an unfortunate yes. I have attached (and still sometimes attach) unnecessary strings to generosity, preconditions that God has not set or approved, in an attempt to control the result of my generosity rather than giving in obedience and leaving the outcome to God.

Uff. That's an uncomfortable confession. Perhaps you've done the same? We often have the best of intentions in wanting to be the best possible stewards of the resources God has entrusted to us, whether we are giving to an organization or to an individual. But what if the control we are trying to exert for fear of making "bad" use of God's money isn't always aligned with what God asks of us?

Scripture has a lot to say about generosity; namely, we are to freely share and to actively care for widows, orphans, and those in difficult situations (see Luke 12:33; Galatians 6:2; 1 John 3:17; Hebrews 13:16). While being good stewards of our resources is an important part of generosity, I've learned that it is the *obedience* in giving that is my responsibility. How those resources are ultimately used (or not) is between the recipient and God.

And even if I don't see an immediate "return" on my generosity, I don't know what's at work in a person's heart or the seeds of faith I might have planted or watered. After all, Jesus healed all ten lepers, knowing only one would return to thank him (see Luke 17:11-19). I've often wondered about the remaining nine. Did they come to know Jesus at a later date? Did Jesus' generosity without expectation start them on a journey that led to their accepting Jesus as Savior?

Eventually, my wondering about those remaining lepers led me to the following questions: What if I treated generosity as Jesus treated healing those lepers? What if I approached giving (especially small amounts) with a no-strings-attached attitude, being obedient in my giving and leaving the impact and results to God? What if I leaned into the reality that—for some of us—faith in God is a years-long journey with dozens of small nudges at divinely appointed moments along the way? Could I focus on loving people and let God handle their souls? The answer is a resounding *yes*!

Some of my family's generosity is specifically reserved for our church and other ministries, but some of it is purposefully no strings attached. We'll slip it anonymously to a family needing mattresses. We help buy school supplies for an elementary school with a high free- and reduced-lunch percentage. We give it to people and places that don't have a 501(c)3 tax-deductible status because we see a need. There are no strings, no expectations, no requirements attached to that generosity. We are obedient to God, and we entrust him with the outcome. While we are thoughtful and prayerful about how and to whom we give, I don't know—for sure—how every penny of those funds is used. And do you know what? It no longer bothers me. My job is obedience in the face of God's sovereignty.

Heavenly Father, we recognize that every penny in our accounts, every asset in our names, every skill set and talent is a gift from you. Thank you for entrusting us with resources that we can use to love and serve those around us. Use us to draw others toward you through obedient, no-strings-attached generosity. Release us from temptation to control every last penny, understanding that what you might be doing is beyond what we can currently see. Amen.

For Reflection:

Prayerfully consider how you've attached an outcome or expectation to your generosity. In what ways can you entrust God with results and keep your own focus on obedience?

Sacred Rhythms:

Keep a small amount of cash on your person, asking God how to give it away this week. Watch for a way to bless someone, no strings attached.

While being good stewards is an important part of generosity, it is the obedience in giving that is our responsibility. How those resources are used is between the recipient and God.

DAY 28

Our Words Matter

The tongue can bring death or life;
those who love to talk will reap the consequences.

PROVERBS 18:21

I (KENDRA) HAVE BEEN FRIENDS WITH JULIE long enough to see her extravagant complimenting of others. I first noticed it when we were in an elevator—usually a quiet experience, but Julie smiled at the woman beside us and told her she loved her shoes.

The woman looked pleasantly surprised as she thanked Julie and told her where she got them. After we exited the elevator, Julie explained to me that she's decided to call out the good things she sees throughout her day; whether it involves a friend or a stranger makes no difference.

"The world is hard enough. I'd like to notice the good. I'm calling it extravagant complimenting," she said with a laugh.

And years later, she continues this habit of speaking up when she sees something worthy of a genuinely kind comment. No matter where we are or what we are doing, she will stop and take the time to sincerely compliment someone. I love to watch how it always brings the person a small measure of joy and connection.

Being extravagant with compliments is good, but it's just one of many ways to be generous with our words.

When I was a little girl, my dad always told me how wise I was. Not smart. Not pretty. But wise. He said my name meant the "knowing woman," and he would often call me that. Now, as an adult, I see the confidence that his words gave me. I loved school and learning new things, and I believe it was partly because my dad had always told me I was wise. It wasn't just lip service either. He would say things he believed about my sisters and me. He was careful in how he spoke to us, reminding us of the unique God-given gifts he believed we'd each been given. He was always generous with his words of affirmation, calling out specific things that he was proud of, loved about us, or could see the potential for in the future.

It's a habit and skill I now use with my own kids. As my children have grown into teenagers and stand on the brink of adulthood, I find it even more important. It's an exciting and scary time of unknown futures but with almost limitless possibility. Sometimes, they are excited, talking about their dreams for the future; other days, they are unsure about what they want to do or what path to take. In both instances, I am quick to cheer them on. To talk through the challenges. To call out what I see as good. To remind them of the skills they've worked hard to attain and those they are still mastering. And even to encourage them in the things they still may need to accomplish.

Being generous with our words isn't only being positive for positivity's sake, but genuine, and honest, and kind. Through it all, I remind my children that no matter what, their dad and I will forever be in their corner. Forever their biggest cheerleaders. I want to be so generous with my words that there is no question about how much I love, believe in, and support them.

Maybe you, too, find it easy to be generous in speaking of others. But even if we've never had anyone cheering us on, either as a child or now as an adult, we get to choose our words in our relationships with others. We get to choose to be generous in our lives today. Just as Julie trained herself to be an extravagant complimenter, we can all learn the habit of being generous with our words.

The Bible talks a lot about our words—and never more clearly than when we are reminded in Proverbs that the tongue can bring life or death, for us or for those around us. And those who love to talk will reap the consequences. But what *are* the consequences? It depends on how we speak.

If we use our words to build others up, encourage them, or even lovingly correct them, we'll reap the consequences of those words in our relationships. We'll most likely find others interacting with us in a similar way—loving, kind, and encouraging.

But the opposite is true as well. Suppose we speak carelessly, tearing others down, talking angrily, or gossiping. In that case, we will reap the consequences of our harsh words with others responding in the same way, and our relationships will suffer as a result.

Words can bring forth death or life, in simple and yet profound ways. But the good news is, whether we have already been using our words wisely or have struggled in the past, we all have a choice going forward in how we will use our speech today and in the future. Even now, we can choose to be generous in how we speak. To strangers. To our family members. To our coworkers. To anyone we come in contact with today.

It may take time and practice, but with God's help, we can bring forth life with our words.

Lord, thank you for giving us wisdom regarding our words. Help us be generous with how we speak to others, willing to offer encouragement, kindness, and even correction in ways that show love toward those around us. If we struggle to use our words to bring forth life, convict us, and give us the wisdom to know when to speak, when to listen, and what to say in each situation that will bring life, not death, to our relationships. Please help us start a new habit of using our words to bring life. When we mess up, give us the courage to admit it and start again. We love you. Thank you for loving us. Amen.

For Reflection:

How have you used your words to bring forth death, and how have you used them to bring forth life? Where may you still need to practice using your words generously?

Sacred Rhythms:

Speak life to someone today, whether by complimenting them extravagantly, encouraging them, or lovingly offering wisdom.

We can choose to be generous in how we speak. To strangers. To our family members. To our coworkers. To anyone we come in contact with today. With God's help, we can bring forth life with our words.

DAY 29

A Budget of Blessing

Most of all, love each other as if your life depended on it. Love makes up for practically anything. Be quick to give a meal to the hungry, a bed to the homeless—cheerfully. Be generous with the different things God gave you, passing them around so all get in on it: if words, let it be God's words; if help, let it be God's hearty help. That way, God's bright presence will be evident in everything through Jesus, and he'll *get all the credit as the One mighty in everything—encores to the end of time. Oh, yes!*

1 PETER 4:8-11, MSG

GENEROSITY IS ONE OF THE THINGS that drew me to my husband. We met on a charity mountain climb in Colorado, and although I (Kristin) was attracted to his humor and brilliant blue eyes, his generosity the day after the hike tipped me over the edge. That morning, the hikers and their families met for breakfast. Much to my surprise, Tim picked up the bill for everyone. When I returned to Minnesota, I emailed to thank him for the thoughtful gesture, and that exchange sparked a romance that turned into marriage less than a year later.

From the beginning, we knew that generosity was important to both of us. Even so, when we first joined our finances, Tim was surprised that although my salary was less than his, I'd given a greater percentage of my income to charity. To be fair, I had been living with my brother-in-law, to help out with my niece and nephew, so my living expenses were minimal. I could give more because I needed less—but he was still impressed that I had chosen to give. Seeing it in black and white helped him to rethink his own approach to giving. Together, creating habits around generosity became a cornerstone in our marriage and finances.

While I'm more likely to be led by my heartstrings in my giving, Tim is better at developing a plan. One year, we created a "blessing budget," something others might call a family giving fund. The idea was to automatically shift funds into an account each month, adding to it over time, to be used for making donations and helping with others' needs. Though we didn't start with much, over time, that small act of faithfulness multiplied. Years later, scrolling through the carbon copies of checks offers beautiful reminders of God's faithfulness in meeting the needs of others through that blessing budget: car repairs, rent, medical or electric bills, plane tickets for someone who was homesick to see their family, a new dishwasher, gifts for kids at Christmastime, and food for those experiencing homelessness.

It's been lovely to witness how God uses these small habits of faithfulness to prompt ripple effects that go much further than we could have imagined. Several years ago, we anonymously helped a young couple at our church who had been experiencing financial difficulties. Years later, my husband was chatting with someone who mentioned how inspired the couple had been by the generosity they'd received. Now that they were back on their feet, they were following our example—quietly and without fanfare helping others in the faith community.

Our giving encourages others to do the same because those who have received help when they desperately need it know how much it matters. I remember my own experience as a new mom—sleep-deprived and at my wit's end. I gratefully received enchiladas, a double recipe of chunky brownies, and many other meals dropped off by friends and family. It was their generosity that spurred me to participate in meal trains for others since then. Perhaps it's only when we've been on the receiving end of generosity that we can truly appreciate the beauty of giving, in the same way that experiencing deep sadness helps us understand great joy. As with those long-ago meals that arrived when I needed them most, my gratitude has often fueled my desire to help others.

As Christians, we know that the greatest act of generosity is the gift of salvation. John 3:16 reminds us that God so loved the world that he *gave*. He gave us his Son, knowing that we were sinful people. This act of mercy, of unlooked-for generosity, is what our faith hinges on. Generosity is the guiding principle in our Christian faith, and it is evident throughout the Bible in ways small and large. In fact, 1 Peter reminds us that we are called to love others as though our lives depended on it—because as members of the family of God and colaborers in the body of Christ, they do. If one of us suffers, we all do. If one of us benefits, we all do.

In God's economy, abundance—not scarcity—is the guiding principle. When we set aside a little something for others through a blessing budget, our small act of obedience can have eternal implications. The truth is that even though we have helped others, we've gained much more in return. On days when life feels hard or God feels far away, I can look back at those carbon copies of checks and my simple list and marvel at how we've witnessed God work in the lives of others. Partnering with God is one of the best ways to gain a front-row seat to his goodness and faithfulness.

Lord, thank you for loving us so much that you gave your Son. Help us mirror your generosity by using our resources to help others in tangible and intangible ways. Give us a heart of wisdom and discernment so we can implement habits of generosity in our daily lives. Amen.

For Reflection:

In what ways have you benefited from someone else's generosity? How does receiving God's grace and mercy encourage us to extend generosity to others?

Sacred Rhythms:

Put together a plan for a blessing budget. Then, begin setting aside funds—even small amounts—to use toward helping others.

In God's economy, abundance is the guiding principle. When we set aside something for others, our small act of obedience can have eternal implications.

DAY 30

Coach Kyle

The generous will prosper; those who refresh others will themselves be refreshed.

PROVERBS 11:25

WHEN OUR SON ABRAM entered high school, he wanted to join the soccer team. Since he had been an avid club player, we weren't surprised. He attended open practices all summer, and as August rolled around and we signed him up for tryouts, we were surprised to see how many other young men wanted to be on the team: over a hundred of them, all vying for a spot.

On the one hand, it was great to have so many kids wanting to be involved in the sport, but the downfall was that there simply wouldn't be enough spots on the four teams for everyone, and the coaching staff was limited—only one coach per team. After the week of tryouts, my husband called me on his way home from picking up Abram.

"Hey, Kendra, what would you think if I offered to volunteer as the assistant coach for Abram's team?" he asked.

"I think that's a great idea. Is he okay with it?" I responded.

"Yes, he is."

"Then I think you should do it."

"But it'll mean I'll need to leave the office early every day to get there for practice by four p.m., and there'll be games in the evenings."

"Okay, I'm fine with that. I think this is important, and you should do it."

Spurred by my encouragement, he emailed the head coach. A week later, with a background check completed, he was on the field for the season's second game.

Over the next month and a half, I watched Kyle work with the young men each day, helping to teach them game skills and encourage them. And he loved every minute of it.

But something more came from the time he gave to be there every day. He got to know the young men. He built relationships and supported kids who could use more positive role models in their lives. He offered rides after practice and games to boys who needed them. I observed how he'd connect after every game, win or lose, telling the boys they did a good job, calling each one by name. "Thanks, Coach," I'd hear as I walked across the field, waiting for all the kids to disperse before approaching him.

Kyle was in his element, in a place where he was thriving and using his God-given talents. There were sacrifices on our part, but the purpose he gained was worth it. He was refreshed by offering refreshment to others, as Proverbs promises. A joy was restored where stress had recently been living. Fun came back into his life in a way it had been lacking. He loved and felt so passionate about seeing the young men succeed, both on and off the field.

Were there challenges? Of course. Some days, kids had bad attitudes. There were unfair calls during games. Riding a school bus home from an away game late at night after losing isn't very fun. Sometimes, the boys argued, and they didn't always care for the correction or direction Kyle and the other coach offered. Relationships can be messy. But that's all a part of the experience. Sacrificing your time is just that: a sacrifice. And yet, the benefits far outweigh the troublesome parts. In Kyle's case, he told me at the end of the season that he couldn't wait until next fall.

We can be generous in many ways, but giving of our time might be one of the most valuable ways we can love others well. Life is busy, and we often observe people wearing their busyness as a badge of honor, a measure of importance. But I can't find anywhere in Scripture that tells me busyness, just for the sake of busyness, is good.

And sometimes, our full schedules can keep us from what God asks of us. Yes, changing our priorities may require a sacrifice of our time. But what if it birthed a new passion inside of you? What if you discovered a new purpose through the giving of your time? What if you made God-ordained connections to others as a result of your sacrifice?

And what if, when you said yes, you were refreshed by the refreshing of others? Because everything that God calls us to do will also benefit others, showing them his love while reminding us of our purpose, which is often found in the time we take to love and be loved.

Some people around you may think you're crazy to be so generous with your time. It often goes against the grain of what we feel we should be doing. But relationships aren't a way to tally productivity.

Kyle gave up time from his job to volunteer with the team. He didn't see any monetary gain from that time—in fact, just the opposite. Yet God provided, in all the ways that mattered most.

And Kyle found, as we all may, that being generous with our time isn't really much of a sacrifice at all—not when we begin to see all God does in and through our obedience to him. He honors our commitment. The peace he gives, the joy, the connection with him and with the people around us—it's worth the sacrifice of time. And maybe our new pursuit will be just the thing we were looking for all along.

Lord, thank you for all the ways you have been generous to us. Help us to notice and give thanks. Show us where we can be generous with our time this week. Nudge us to listen to your Holy Spirit's leading and take the time we need to be there for someone else. Show us the purpose we have when we use our time wisely and generously on behalf of others. We love you, Jesus. Amen.

For Reflection:

When was the last time you were generous with your time? How did it make you feel? Where may God currently be asking you to give of your time? How might it be tied to a purpose God has for you?

Sacred Rhythms:

Be generous with your time by spending it with someone God brings across your path today.

Being generous with our time isn't really much of a sacrifice at all—not when we begin to see all God does in and through our obedience to him.

DAY 31

A Community of Generosity

Let us consider how to stir up one another to love and good works, not neglecting to meet together, as is the habit of some, but encouraging one another, and all the more as you see the Day drawing near.

HEBREWS 10:24-25, ESV

OPENING THE DOOR, I stepped inside and stomped my feet, shivering as snow clung to the soles of my boots. Saying hello to an acquaintance, I quickly headed from the entryway toward the main space.

"Hey, Kristin," my friend Jenny greeted me as she completed the final touches for the event. The room was cavernous, full of big windows and wide-open spaces. At the front, a table full of Dixie cups, a basket of crackers, and some paperwork had been positioned next to a stage. I breathed a sigh of relief when I spotted my friend Steph among the tidy rows of chairs rapidly filling with other women and beelined for the seat next to hers.

It was the first meeting of Leaven, a group-giving initiative involving women in our local community. A few months earlier, Jenny had introduced the idea on social media. The rules were simple: We would meet quarterly for an hour. Each woman would bring $100 to be given away (or, she could split that amount with someone else). Before the meeting, members would submit nominations for individuals, families, or organizations who could use a helping hand. During the meeting, we would prayerfully choose a nominee and collectively give the total amount to the recipient. Lastly, we'd close with Communion and prayer.

More than forty women had said, "I'm in!" And at our first meeting, the fruit of that faithfulness was in motion. After praying, Jenny invited those who had nominated someone to tell us more about their circumstances. All nominees had experienced life-threatening health concerns, seemingly insurmountable financial difficulties, or other heartbreaking challenges. Silent tears slipped down my cheeks and landed on my jacket as I listened to the pain and heartache of those in our community.

After we each submitted our choice anonymously, Jenny tallied the votes while we sat quietly, juice and crackers in hand.

The person we chose was about my age, someone I'd met and chatted with in the past, someone I saw regularly on social media. I knew part of their story, but I felt a fierce hope as I thought about what our collective $3,600 would mean for them and their family.

Before we left our Leaven gathering, we joined together in a circle. What other prayer requests did we have? Jenny wanted to know. Who else needed prayer in our community? I kept my gaze steadily on the floor, trying not to let tears spill over once again as I heard even more stories of heartache, worry, and pain. As Jenny prayed, I felt simultaneously convicted and encouraged by her simple words. How many times had I walked past someone in pain without realizing it? How could I be more open to the Holy Spirit's lead in helping them, even if only in prayer? How could I continue to partner with others to meet the tangible needs of those around me?

Hebrews 10:24-25 talks about stirring one another to love and good works, meeting together, and encouraging one another. But the verse that precedes these two is just as important: "Let us hold fast the confession of our hope without wavering, for he who promised is faithful" (Hebrews 10:23, ESV). It's because of our faithfulness and our hope in Jesus that we can take that vertical relationship (looking toward Jesus) and move into a horizontal relationship (spreading his love in the world).

Often, it's our friendships, our relationships with others, or the community at large that help spur us on to do more for the Kingdom of God. As members of the body of Christ, meeting together reminds us that we are working together as one for a common goal: to be the hands and feet of Jesus in this world by using our time, money, and other resources to take part in the living testimony of God's faithfulness to us and others.

You and I are witnesses and participants in the good news that Jesus has for all of us, and we have work to accomplish in this world. As Saint Teresa of Avila is said to have written,

Christ has no body but yours,
No hands, no feet on earth but yours,
Yours are the eyes with which he looks
Compassion on this world,
Yours are the feet with which he walks to do good,
Yours are the hands, with which he blesses all the world. . . .
Christ has no body now on earth but yours.

As colaborers with Christ, it is our sacred honor and duty to carry out the gospel's good news in this world. Our hands and feet do this work, yet we can go further when we work together.

There's a concept called "body doubling" that reminds us of the impact of working side by side. Often used as a productivity tool, body doubling occurs when someone works alongside another person as they complete homework or household tasks. The idea is that it helps the person trying to complete a task to stay motivated and accountable. When I declutter my house, I often turn on decluttering experts who are doing the same thing. As they work their way through their belongings, I work my way through mine. Even though we are separated by distance and time, listening to them sort through the mess of their lives while I simultaneously sort through mine is encouraging, helpful, and motivating.

The same is true for our Christian walk. How many times has someone else's kindness spurred our own? How often have we invited someone to join us because we, too, were once outsiders who were invited in? And how does seeing generosity in action—seeing others working toward the everyday goodness of the gospel—nudge us to be a little more generous than we might otherwise have been?

Jenny chose *Leaven* for the name of our gathering because of Luke 13:20-21, in which Jesus compares the Kingdom of God to the ordinary, everyday task of making bread: "What else is the Kingdom of God like? It is like the yeast a woman used in making bread. Even though she put only a little yeast in three measures of flour, it permeated every part of the dough." Though we may believe we have little to offer, together, we can have an impact that reaches far beyond ourselves as individuals. Our offering—no matter how small—can be used toward a collective good with long-lasting, far-reaching implications for the Kingdom of God.

Lord, thank you that we can be the hands and feet of Jesus in this world, working side by side to spread your love and grace. Help us to seek out opportunities to join with others to help our generosity go even further. Amen.

For Reflection:

Why is it important to consider the impact of community on our generosity? How does Scripture influence our approach to collective generosity?

Sacred Rhythms:

Consider how you can partner with others to be the hands and feet of Jesus. Today, take one step toward collective generosity. Examples: Volunteer at church or in your community, pool resources to help someone, or organize a meal train.

How many times has someone else's kindness spurred our own? How does seeing generosity in action nudge us to be a little more generous than we might otherwise have been?

DAY 32

For Further Reflection

1. What stood out to you about generosity this week? What surprised or inspired you? What tested or challenged you?

2. What insights did you gain through this week's fast from unnecessary spending so you could be more generous?

3. How do you demonstrate generosity well, and where can you work to improve?

____

____

____

____

____

Lord, thank you for the opportunities to be generous toward others—with our time, resources, words, thoughts, and actions. May we ponder your love and kindness for us, and may we remember we can never outgive you. You are a good, generous God. May we have wisdom to go throughout our days looking for big and small ways to share generously with those around us. And may we be obedient to the nudging of your Spirit. We love you. Thank you for loving us. Amen.

WEEK 6

FREEDOM

Sunday–Saturday

DAY 33

Freedom in Christ

Christ has truly set us free. Now make sure that you stay free, and don't get tied up again in slavery to the law.

GALATIANS 5:1

I (KENDRA) REMEMBER STANDING ON THE STAGE, proud to receive a large ribbon signifying all the Scriptures I'd memorized the past year in my girls' group. I wasn't a terribly athletic or skilled child, but I could memorize Scriptures. It felt good to be recognized as the girl who'd learned the most verses throughout the year.

As an adult, that memory work has served me well. Scripture often comes to mind as I ask God for wisdom or guidance or talk with him about my day. God and his Word have always been a part of my life, and my conscious thoughts swirl naturally around him because I was told as a child that God wanted to talk with me, and I was encouraged to go to him with every concern. My knowledge of Scripture has become part of who I am. And for a long time, I felt pride about how much I knew and how familiar the verses were to me.

No one understood the potential for pride in our achievements more than Paul. He says in Philippians 3:4-8,

> If someone else thinks they have reasons to put confidence in the flesh, I have more: circumcised on the eighth day, of the people of Israel, of the tribe of Benjamin, a Hebrew of Hebrews; in regard to the law, a Pharisee; as for zeal, persecuting the church; as for righteousness based on the law, faultless. But whatever were gains to me I now consider loss for the sake of Christ. What is more, I consider everything a loss because of the surpassing worth of knowing Christ Jesus my Lord, for whose sake I have lost all things. I consider them garbage, that I may gain Christ. (NIV)

I, too, knew all the rules of our faith. I knew how I was supposed to behave, how I was supposed to act. But what I lacked was the decision to truly live it out. Whatever gains I thought I had meant nothing compared to knowing Christ and following his ways.

Knowing Scripture is not the same as living it and applying it to my life. It can be easy to memorize Scripture or write it out on note cards. It's another thing to look at your life and see where God's Word can correct, challenge, or even change your thoughts, habits, and behaviors—to allow Jesus to be Lord. But that is precisely what he asks of us.

It sounds counterintuitive, but there is freedom in making Jesus the Lord of your life. This is good news for all of us. Whether we grew up in the faith or came to know Jesus as adults, we are all free to come and follow him now, just as we are. No one is left out. The freedom to know Christ is available to each of us, because it is Christ who sets us free. Not we ourselves. Not our behaviors or actions. A change in behavior certainly follows a life lived in pursuit of Jesus, but it doesn't need to precede it. Jesus tells us to come just the way we are.

There's no greater freedom than that—to know you are fully loved, accepted, and known. To know that there is no need to prove ourselves to God with our accomplishments. We accept that freedom and don't allow ourselves to get tied up again in the law. Instead, we use our freedom to love God and those around us.

Paul knew what it meant to make Jesus Lord, and this is attainable for us too. There are no super Christians. We're it—imperfect, flawed, messy. But if we are totally reliant on Christ and surrendered to him, we will see amazing things happen. Despite Paul's past achievements, his life really wasn't that influential—not in any lasting way—until he surrendered to Christ.

Jesus calls us to follow him as Paul did: to set aside our own efforts, know him intimately, read his words, and follow him in full surrender.

When we do this, we'll find the freedom only he can give.

This Week's Fasting Focus

This week, we want to be mindful of the freedoms afforded us daily. We can so easily take for granted necessities like food and clean drinking water as well as various comforts that we enjoy throughout our days but that don't come so easily for many others worldwide.

Did you know that currently about two billion people in our world do not have access to clean and safe drinking water?[1] Or that 900 million people face severe food insecurity?[2] This is shocking and alarming, especially considering how much we've been given.

So, this week, let's choose a comfort to forgo. For example, let's drink only water or give up caffeine, alcohol, meat, or sugar—whatever comfort we reach for each day without even thinking. May it be a reminder that something we have freedom to enjoy regularly, others around the world do not have easy access to. Each time we deny ourselves, let's say a prayer for people worldwide who are living without the basic necessities, let alone the comforts we enjoy.

Lord, thank you for the freedoms we've been given. May we never take them for granted but instead choose to lay down our rights so we can follow you and serve others in love. We love you, Jesus. Bless our week as we seek to walk in true freedom. Amen.

DAY 34

Freedom Through Grace—for Us and Others

You were called to freedom, brothers. Only do not use your freedom as an opportunity for the flesh, but through love serve one another. For the whole law is fulfilled in one word: "You shall love your neighbor as yourself."

GALATIANS 5:13-14, ESV

I'M NOT A RUNNER. I (Kristin) am more of a reluctant exerciser, seeking activities that will help me be healthy but also let me watch old episodes of *Hoarders* or *Top Chef* to distract myself from what I'm doing. So when three friends asked me to join them in a charity run, I hesitated. Eight miles? On a Saturday morning?

I agreed when they assured me we could walk the course, not run. As I dug deeper into the reason behind the event, I understood why they'd gently pushed me to join them.

The run was to raise money for women trapped in poverty and abuse. Funds were to be earmarked for marginalized young women halfway around the world who were prime targets for human trafficking. The proceeds would help provide safe housing and resources like vocational training. They would also give women access to feminine hygiene products and education about their bodies so they could continue attending school and working.

Freedom from abuse. Freedom from pain. Freedom to flourish. How could I say no?

Along with 172 other women, my three friends and I helped to raise more than $96,000 and logged a combined total of 1,280 miles—all for women we'll never meet.

Those statistics aren't meant to inspire accolades but to encourage you to reconsider what it means to be free. I have experienced the privilege of freedom. I've never felt truly hopeless or helpless, lacking access to education or health care. I've never had to consider whether I should sell my body in exchange for food or shelter. I can dream, create, and live in safety. There's a good chance you can say the same.

Yet *physical* freedom is just one of the freedoms we can experience. A person who abuses alcohol to numb their emotions or chases meaningless relationships to fill a void may be physically free yet in bondage to sin. The deepest, truest freedom comes from knowing Jesus as our Savior. He is the one who provides lasting *spiritual* freedom.

The spiritual freedom Jesus longs to give us reminds me in a small way of the classic childhood game of hide-and-seek. As a child, I remember squeezing myself into the smallest, darkest spaces possible, trying to slow my breath and racing heartbeat and to avoid giggling or giving myself away. While I wanted to win—either by being found last or by hiding so well that I had to call out when my friend gave up—I also wanted to be found. I wanted to emerge from the darkness and rejoin the people I loved. Instead of close spaces and hidden darkness, I longed for the fresh air and freedom of being found. Though that meant losing the game, there was freedom in knowing that somebody cared enough about me to keep looking.

Jesus is the ultimate seeker. He wants to provide the freedom we desperately need because he recognizes its power to change lives. Galatians reminds us that we have been called to freedom, yet it's not something we should hoard for ourselves. As with hide-and-seek, the freedom of Christ's love is our invitation to find others and help bring them into the light. We can use our newfound freedom to love and serve others like Jesus did. Loving our neighbors is more than simply caring for the people who live beside us; it's an awareness that you and I can use our voices and resources to help others experience the same kind of freedom we've experienced.

This freedom is only possible because of the grace and mercy of Jesus. In the Old Testament, the law was the standard God gave Moses, beginning with the Ten Commandments. The laws were intended to set apart God's people from the nations around them and to define what sin was. But by the time Jesus arrived, religious leaders had added to the law, and it had become incredibly burdensome.

The freedom we experience, thanks to the grace and mercy of Jesus and his sacrifice, was a fulfillment, not a replacement, for Old Testament laws. Jesus reassured skeptical religious leaders of his purpose: "Don't misunderstand why I have come. I did not come to abolish the law of Moses or the writings of the prophets. No, I came to accomplish their purpose" (Matthew 5:17).

In other words, the law was meant to reflect what was in people's hearts, but it did not have the power to *change* their hearts. Jesus, on the other hand, embodied both truth (law) and grace (mercy) (see John 1:17). Jesus' sacrifice on the cross for our sins meant that the law was fulfilled, establishing a new covenant with him. Our freedom from sin doesn't mean that we are no longer governed by moral law but that we instead have the freedom that comes from walking in the Spirit. Romans 8:1-4 reminds us of this truth:

> There is therefore now no condemnation for those who are in Christ Jesus. For the law of the Spirit of life has set you free in Christ Jesus from the law of sin and death. For God has done what the law, weakened by the flesh, could not do. By sending his own Son in the likeness of sinful flesh and for sin, he condemned sin in the flesh, in order that the righteous requirement of the law might be fulfilled in us, who walk not according to the flesh but according to the Spirit. (ESV)

Because we have experienced a heart change (grace) and are no longer simply following the rules (law), sin does not rule us now: "Sin is no longer your master, for you no longer live under the requirements of the law. Instead, you live under the freedom of God's grace" (Romans 6:14).

Our freedom doesn't give us the license to live however we want. Instead, because of the influence of the Holy Spirit, we are inspired to love God and love others (see 2 Corinthians 3:17). We are not trying to earn our holiness but instead to share the grace and mercy we have received. Our firsthand experience with freedom empowers us to share its life-changing power by helping others.

Lord Jesus, thank you for the freedom we experience through salvation, which is only made possible by your sacrifice on the cross. Help us to use our freedom to love you and to love others. May we continue to find ways to shine light into the darkness, helping those around us to find you and the freedom you bring. Amen.

For Reflection:

How is spiritual freedom different from physical freedom?

How can you use your freedom to help others find freedom?

Sacred Rhythms:

Research and support an organization helping others attain freedom, whether by utilizing your resources or standing alongside them in prayer.

Loving our neighbors is more than simply caring for the people beside us; it's an awareness that we can use our voices and resources to help others experience freedom.

DAY 35

Freedom from Worry

Be anxious for nothing, but in everything by prayer and supplication, with thanksgiving, let your requests be made known to God; and the peace of God, which surpasses all understanding, will guard your hearts and minds through Christ Jesus.

PHILIPPIANS 4:6-7, NKJV

"DOES EVERYONE HAVE THEIR AIRTAG? And is it in a zippered pocket so it can't fall out?" I tried to make my questions sound casual and nonchalant as I spread peanut butter across bread. I was prepping lunches for my family before their skiing adventure on a "real" mountain in a Western state instead of the relatively tiny ski hills found in Minnesota.

"Julie, we're going to be fine," Aaron said at the same time that Lizzie asked, "Mom, what do you think is going to happen to us?"

"Well, what if there is an avalanche?" I responded to three incredulous looks from various parts of the kitchen–living room combo of our Vrbo.

"Mom, you know how little snow they've received this early in the season. How would there be an avalanche?" Jon's question was kind rather than dismissive.

Realizing that I was engaging in unreasonable worry, I changed tactics:

"Well, okay. That's true. I'd just feel better if you guys had AirTags. I'll have mine, despite not being on the mountain."

With a bit of grumbling about my overprotective tendencies, my husband and teens hit the slopes, each with a tracking tag tucked into an interior coat pocket.

Was I being ridiculous? Yes. Did I know it intellectually even as my heart wanted to wrap them in Bubble Wrap but was willing to compromise with the trackers? Also yes. Did they humor my worry? A third yes.

I am prone to worry. Three years of law school followed by fifteen years practicing law means if you need someone to anticipate every conceivable worst-case scenario (and several ridiculous ones), I'm your girl! The legal profession is rife with substance abuse, in part—I believe—because we are paid to both anticipate and carry the worries of others.

Unfortunately, we lawyers are not alone in our overactive fretting. We are a nation consumed with worry. Worry has been linked to all the leading causes of death, including heart disease, cancer, lung problems, accidents, cirrhosis, and suicide.[1] An estimated one million workers are absent on an average workday because of stress-related complaints.[2] Add to the list the mental fatigue of nights without sleep and days without peace, and we get a glimpse of the havoc worry plays in destroying the quality and quantity of our lives.

If we let it, worry will hold us in bondage physically, emotionally, and spiritually. With over three hundred Scriptures telling us not to worry or fear, we can be sure that God knows how detrimental worry is to our overall well-being. When we are exhausted and distracted by worry, we diminish our witness and make it difficult for God to use us in bringing the Kingdom of Heaven to earth.

If we proclaim God with our words but continually walk around as a fretting, anxious mess, who will believe us when we say God is good and can be trusted? No one.

And if we are consumed with worry over tomorrow, how will we notice the divine appointments God has placed across our path today? We won't.

Rather than berate ourselves over our tendency toward worry, let's embrace the freedom God offers by forming new habits and a daily (or even hourly or minute-by-minute) choice.

When I find myself starting to fret, I interrupt myself and recite a paraphrase of today's verse accompanied with a quick prayer turning that specific worry to God. I ask him to be with me and my loved ones, and I remind myself of who he is (see Psalm 147:4; Luke 12:7), no matter what (see Psalm 139:7-10). I repeat that process as many times as necessary.

My thought-interrupting prayer looks something like this:

Heavenly Father, you promise that your peace—the peace that surpasses all understanding—is ours for the asking. Thank you for giving me your peace. You know all the details of this situation, and I hand every part of it back to you. You know the stars in the sky by name and count the hairs on our heads. May your Holy Spirit be tangibly close, may your will prevail, and may this challenge be used to bring you glory. Amen.

There have been days and circumstances in which I've looped through that process a dozen times (or more) in an hour, and that's okay. Over time, recognizing and interrupting our worries with prayer and Scripture builds new habits and allows us to embrace the freedom of God's peace, even when life is uncertain and hard. Of course, this is not my only prayer about the situation; this is simply my worry-interrupter. I repeat this prayer mantra as many times as necessary to change my thought patterns, but I also take the time to pray in more detail about each situation during my regular prayer times.

I also use this prayer on behalf of other people. Rather than relying on well-intentioned clichés that can do more harm than good (such as everything happens for a reason, God doesn't give us more than we can handle, what doesn't kill you makes you stronger, time heals all wounds), we can use our prayer mantra via text or note card to invoke the unsurpassable peace of God to rest on our loved ones, even as we delve deeper into prayer on their behalf privately or later.

An important caveat: In some cases, anxiety is a diagnosis and is a legitimate medical condition that often involves medicine or other interventions. There is zero shame or condemnation to be found in one's battle against anxiety nor in combining prayer with God-gifted medical knowledge and techniques.

Friends, God wants to set you free from worry. This freedom can be both instantaneous and also a journey, depending upon our personalities, the patterns we've developed, the situation, and even the day. God gives grace, even as we do the hard work of interrupting those patterns.

Heavenly Father, thank you for freeing us from the overwhelming bondage of worry. Thank you for the gift of your peace when ours is flimsy. Help us interrupt patterns and habits of unhealthy worry so that we can be our healthiest selves physically, emotionally, and spiritually. Amen.

For Reflection:

What are you prone to worry over or about to the point of it becoming an unhealthy pattern or habit in your life?

Sacred Rhythms:

Create your own prayer mantra based on today's Scripture to help interrupt the cycle of worry. (You are welcome to use mine if it's helpful.)

Interrupting our worries with prayer and Scripture builds new habits and allows us to embrace the freedom of God's peace.

DAY 36

Freedom in Surrender

Seek the Kingdom of God above all else, and live righteously, and he will give you everything you need.

MATTHEW 6:33

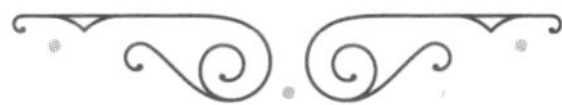

BEFORE WE MOVED TO OUR CURRENT HOME, we had a house in an incredibly safe neighborhood. It was our dream house when we bought it, and we thought we'd never move. But God has a way of changing our hearts and our dreams to be more in line with his purposes. So we moved. Our current house, situated in the heart of our city, has much more traffic and transient people coming through on a regular basis. It's not necessarily bad, just very different.

Here's something I (Kendra) am a bit embarrassed to admit: I've always dealt with a lot of fear. At times, it's consumed me. I was freakishly scared as a child. God has helped me work through my fears and has set me free from many of them, but one area had hung on. I have always been afraid of the dark, of night. As a child living at home, I'd beg my sisters to let me sleep with them.

The house Kyle and I previously lived in had an alarm system that I'd triple-check at night. I slept with my glasses on and my pillow propped. Most nights, I slept very lightly and would wake up at the slightest noise.

But after we moved, trusting God's leading, and surrendering our will and our dreams of what we thought was the next step . . . I slept well the first night. Really well. I thought it was curious, maybe just a fluke. But the next night, I slept well again, and the next. And every night since then. We have no alarm system in this house. I don't triple-check the locks at night. I take my glasses off when I go to bed, and I often sleep with my back to the door. Maybe this doesn't sound like a big deal, but for someone who's never slept well, it's nothing short of miraculous.

As I've processed what it means to surrender our lives and our freedom, I've realized that God never told me I would sleep well in this new house. And honestly, I never even considered it as we were looking for a new place to live. I've just always lived with troubled sleep. I did not realize God would give me such peace in this new space. Yet that is precisely what I have received.

When we seek the Kingdom of God above all else, he meets our needs in ways that may surprise us. I wonder: What blessing could be waiting for *you* on the other side of surrender? What pain could God ease? What joy could he offer? What fear could he cause to subside? We often think about surrender as giving something up, yet we gain so much more than we could ever imagine when surrendering our freedom, or will, to God's plan.

Giving up our freedom goes against what many of us have been taught, especially if we grew up in a first-world country. We talk a lot about our rights and our freedom and about protecting them at any cost. But that is not what God asks of us. In fact, it's just the opposite. God tells us to lay down our life and our will for others.

That can feel hard—unless we know that God's plan, his purpose, is better than anything we could come up with on our own. It's not so difficult when we know we can trust in who he is and when we remember his kindness, his compassion, and the love he extends to us. As God's Word says, "We know what real love is because Jesus gave up his life for us. So we also ought to give up our lives for our brothers and sisters" (1 John 3:16).

He laid down his life for us. And now he asks us to do the same for him and for others.

But this is a process, a continual laying down, day after day. It is a *choice* to surrender. God never coerces or forces us. But it is what God wants from each of us. Rather than clinging to our rights and freedoms in this world, we are to seek God's Kingdom above any other kingdom, the true Kingdom that will last beyond time and space and into eternity. We must have a heavenly perspective instead of just an earthly one.

Surrender is not always easy. But anytime I find myself missing my old home, every time I ache for the neighbors I had and the memories of that place, I recall how well I sleep now. How only God could have removed that fear I'd had for all those years—so long that I'd stopped asking him to take it away. I'm reminded that I'd much rather be where he wants me than to be anywhere else.

Sacrifice and surrender are hard, but they are worth it. It's one way we experience God's Kingdom right here on earth. The truth is, we may never know until we lay down our will what other freedoms may open up to us with a simple yes, a simple surrender.

Seek God's Kingdom, and all these things will be given to you. It's not just a command. It's a promise.

What might you find on the other side of surrender?

Lord, thank you for the freedom we can find in surrendering to you. Thank you for being a good God—one who is trustworthy and true. One thing we can be sure of as we lay down our rights is that you always have our best in mind. Although the process may be painful, we know that a greater reward will be awaiting us. Please help us seek your Kingdom first above any other kingdom of this world. We love you. Amen.

For Reflection:

What is God asking you to surrender in this season of your life? What might you gain on the other side of surrender?

Sacred Rhythms:

To grow your heart of surrender, choose one small way you can lay down your will before God today.

When we seek the Kingdom of God above all else, he meets our needs in ways that may surprise us. What blessing could be waiting for *you* on the other side of surrender?

DAY 37

Freedom from Shame

The Word gave life to everything that was created, and his life brought light to everyone. The light shines in the darkness, and the darkness can never extinguish it.

JOHN 1:4-5

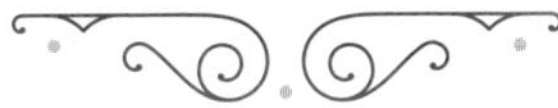

FACE IN FLAMES, I (Kristin) shifted quietly in the living room chair but felt no relief. My husband and I sat silently, uneasily, while the other people in the room discussed current events. The three of them were part of an older generation, and when they began to casually throw out stereotypes and intolerant language, I felt miserable.

On the one hand, I had been taught to respect my elders. And in many ways, I did in this case. These were people I knew and treasured. On the other hand, I found their words unloving and seemingly at odds with who I thought them to be.

I spared a glance at my husband, who looked equally uncomfortable. Together, we quickly—mercifully—were able to change the subject.

But a part of me felt silenced—by their age, by my youth, and by the worry that I'd start a fight or become overly emotional. Later, I felt ashamed. Why couldn't I speak up and tell them how I really felt? What was I afraid of?

Brené Brown, in her book *Daring Greatly*, defines shame as "the intensely painful feeling or experience of believing that we are flawed and therefore unworthy of love and belonging." One of the major markers of shame is our inability to name it or talk about it. As Brown notes, "Shame derives its power from being unspeakable."[1]

Often, the things we struggle to name or speak aloud are our greatest sources of shame. While guilt will tell us, "I did something bad," shame convinces us that we *are* bad. While guilt tells us, "I lied," shame will heap on more pain by telling us that we *are* a liar. When I didn't immediately speak up, guilt recognized that I felt afraid, but shame told me, "You are a coward." Shame takes our mistakes and missteps and turns them into character flaws, and in turn, we take that pain and bury it deep inside us.

Yet Jesus has come to free us, and the miracle of grace is that it covers all things, not just the polite things we're okay with talking about in public. As 1 John 3:20 reminds us, "Even if we feel guilty, God is greater than our feelings, and he knows everything." In other words, there is nothing we can do that God doesn't already know about or can't forgive. He is greater than any feeling we may have—including shame—and we can always seek his help to overcome it. We often show up to Jesus with our hat in hand, unsure of our welcome, even though we have been directed to approach God confidently, understanding that we will receive mercy and find grace in his presence (see Hebrews 4:16). The grace and mercy of Jesus shed light on the dark places in our lives—especially those cloaked in shame—and bring the freedom we desperately need.

The light of Jesus illuminates the darkest places in our hearts. John describes Jesus as a light source that can never be extinguished. But the wonder of being his children is that when we choose to follow him, we also become light-bearers:

> God, who said, "Let there be light in the darkness," has made this light shine in our hearts so we could know the glory of God that is seen in the face of Jesus Christ. We now have this light shining in our hearts, but we ourselves are like fragile clay jars containing this great treasure. This makes it clear that our great power is from God, not from ourselves.
>
> 2 CORINTHIANS 4:6-7

Thanks to Jesus, we bear the light of his grace and mercy inside us—not because of our strength or power but because of his. This means that the same light that Jesus brought radiates from us, and even the darkest secrets and shame we hold inside are not strong enough to overcome the light and love of Jesus.

When we shed light on the truth, we battle against the darkness. As 1 John 1:7 reminds us, "If we are living in the light, as God is in the light, then we have fellowship with each other, and the blood of Jesus, his Son, cleanses us from all sin." We often consider "fellowship" to be merely an individual in community with others, but in the original text, the word evoked a deeper communion among the saints.[2] More than a social gathering, fellowship signified a melding of hearts akin to the intimacy of being members of one body, the body of Christ.

Being willing to share our struggles with other believers affirms our connection, but it also brings a profound sense of relief. According to Brené Brown, empathy is one of the greatest ways to combat shame.[3] When we share our burden with someone else and hear the words, "Me too," shame loses its power. And when we overcome shame, we find lasting freedom.

A few years later, I had a similar encounter with unloving speech. This time, I was ready when the person tried to argue why they were right.

"You know, you can probably find a study to back up just about any 'fact,'" I said calmly, "but even if you did, I can't agree. I have a problem with the moral implications of the argument, so I could never agree."

The person listened, and while we agreed to disagree, we left at peace with one another. And I felt okay about it. I felt like I'd found my voice.

Lord Jesus, thank you for your mercy, which has the power to overcome shame. May we always remember that we can confidently approach you, knowing that you are ready and willing to forgive us and to shed light on the darkness in our lives. Help us to seek freedom by overcoming shame. Amen.

For Reflection:

What sins or hidden parts of your life cause you to feel shame? How might it feel to expose those parts of your life to the light of God's love and truth? What would it be like to feel truly free?

Sacred Rhythms:

Write down one thing that causes you shame. Ask Jesus to help you bring light to this dark area. If you feel so inclined, share your burden with a trusted friend.

There is nothing we can do that God doesn't already know about or can't forgive. He is greater than any feeling we may have—including shame.

DAY 38

Freedom for Everyone

Though I am free from all, I have made myself a servant to all.

1 CORINTHIANS 9:19

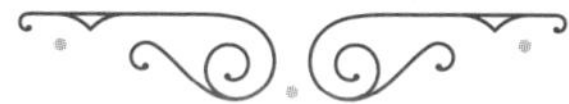

"UM . . . IS THE VOICE IN YOUR HEAD being unfairly mean to you again? Because I think she might be . . ."

My text swooshed off, bouncing off a tower or three before landing in my friend's cell phone. A moment later, those little dots appeared, showing a response was on the way: *"Thanks, Julie. You might be right, and I needed that reminder."*

My shoulders released the tension I didn't realize I was carrying as I read her words, especially with the heart emoji that accompanied it. I love my friend, and I know her well enough to recognize when her inner critic is telling her things that are not true. It's a trap she is prone to fall into when life feels overwhelming. I've learned that a direct question about her inner voice helps reframe her thoughts so she can break free of that spiral. I invite her back into freedom in Christ, and quite frankly, she does the same for me, despite my situation and my freedom looking different from hers.

Freedom. While the physical version of it can arrive in dramatic fashion, with a made-for-TV rescue by a SEAL team or law enforcement, not all liberators wear camouflage or carry guns, and not all freedom is physical. Emotional and spiritual freedom often arrive quietly and without fanfare, following an invitation extended by ordinary people who have found their own freedom in Christ and are willing to carry the offer forward to others.

That's part of our Christian walk: Once we receive freedom from sin, from Old Testament requirements, from condemnation and shame, and from all of the unhealthy ways we allow ourselves to be shackled, we are to use our freedom in loving and serving others rather than for selfish gain. One way we do that is by telling others where to find their own freedom.

A friend tells a story of groceries being left on her doorstep during a particularly difficult season. That extra food, with treats included and accompanied by a written prayer, was physical and spiritual hope. It was a reminder that God was with them and was providing even in hard circumstances, and that their friend was praying on their behalf. It was a reminder of their freedom in Christ and that God was in charge of tomorrow.

I speak frankly with my college-level business law students about what justice is and is not in the context of our legal system. We discuss the interplay of wealth, connections, race, and power with discretion. We talk about whether when leniency for identical crimes is granted more frequently to those with enough resources or the right connections or a lighter skin tone it is actually mercy rather than something more sinister and damaging to our entire society. It is a reminder that people beloved by God have been treated as less important, despite God's clear instruction that not one of us is more important than another. Freedom is for all of us.

When I (finally) confessed to Kendra and Kristin that I've been struggling with short-term memory lapses since the onset of perimenopause and my fears related to it, they began supporting my forgetfulness by (with kindness) reminding me of important upcoming dates related to our ministry and writing. These reminders are without fanfare, shame, or making me feel worse than I already sometimes do. It has been a reminder that our freedom in Christ sometimes means that we are the one receiving physical, emotional, or spiritual care from those around us.

Bringing freedom to others can be as easy as taking the time to notice what another person is struggling with and easing their burden physically or emotionally as we point them toward the ultimate liberator, Jesus. We can meet temporary needs while offering Jesus as true, root-cause freedom.

But it can also feel risky. We might have to speak up when we know someone is being harmed. We might have to decline an invitation to be among the powerful and influential when the policies they create or the decisions they make benefit a carefully chosen few rather than the many. We might have to reconsider our behaviors or ways of thinking, asking Jesus for discernment and wisdom and forgiveness if what we've done to others (or ourselves!) has resulted in emotional, physical, or spiritual bondage rather than freedom.

Freedom might require us to be inviters as well as advocates. And we might be decently good at the one while struggling with the other. That's okay. Our faith journey is a process, not a destination that we'll arrive at this side of heaven. But as part of that journey, we must be willing to advocate and invite others into the same freedom we've found in Jesus.

Heavenly Father, thank you for the freedom found in Jesus' sacrificial death and resurrection. Thank you that we are no longer in bondage to sin, are no longer under the Old Testament covenant, are not subject to condemnation and shame. Thank you for fighting for our freedom. Help us to be advocates and inviters into that same freedom for those around us. May we be people who work alongside Jesus to bring physical and emotional freedom as he extends the greatest gift: spiritual freedom. Amen.

For Reflection:

In what areas have you struggled physically, emotionally, or spiritually before finding freedom in Jesus? In what ways are you still prone to struggle, even knowing that you are free?

Sacred Rhythms:

How can you promote freedom this week, either as an inviter or as an advocate? Watch and listen carefully for opportunities to bring others into freedom.

Emotional and spiritual freedom often arrive quietly and without fanfare, following an invitation extended by ordinary people who have found their own freedom in Christ.

DAY 39

For Further Reflection

1. What stood out to you about freedom this week? What surprised or inspired you? What tested or challenged you?

2. What insights did you gain through this week's fast from a comfort you usually have freedom to enjoy regularly?

3. Where do you walk in freedom, and where can you work to improve?

____

____

____

____

____

Lord, thank you for being the original liberating force in our lives. Thank you for freeing us from the shackles of sin physically, emotionally, and spiritually. Help us recognize where we are living shackled and embrace the freedom you offer, in every area! And may we be people who bring your freedom to those around us. Amen.

HOLY WEEK

HOPE

Palm Sunday–Silent Saturday

DAY 40

Embracing an Eternal Perspective

Trust in the LORD with all your heart and lean not on your own understanding; in all your ways submit to him, and he will make your paths straight.

PROVERBS 3:5-6, NIV

TODAY IS PALM SUNDAY. While it marks the start of Holy Week, a week of both suffering and joy for those of us who know the full Easter story, I (Julie) imagine that the day must have been an amazing, jubilant celebration for those followers of Jesus who were present as he rode through the streets of Jerusalem.

All four Gospel accounts record the triumphal entry, the arrival of Jesus in Jerusalem on the back of a young, never-before-ridden donkey (see Matthew 21:1-17; Mark 11:1-11; Luke 19:29-40; John 12:12-19). His arrival in such a manner fulfilled the prophecy of Zechariah:

> Rejoice greatly, Daughter Zion!
> Shout, Daughter Jerusalem!

> See, your king comes to you,
> righteous and victorious,
> lowly and riding on a donkey,
> on a colt, the foal of a donkey.
>
> ZECHARIAH 9:9, NIV

By arriving in this manner, Jesus publicly claimed his role as the foretold, long-awaited Messiah and King of Israel. And, for a moment, there was rejoicing. People thought his kingship would bring about physical freedom from the very real, violent choke hold of Rome. They expected an earthly deliverance, with Jesus assuming a tangible, earthly reign over a visible, earthly kingdom.

Of course, we know Jesus had something different in mind. We understand how events would unfold over the upcoming week in a way his followers could not and did not understand. Jesus came as our spiritual Messiah, and his victory over sin won a spiritual war against Satan—establishing a Kingdom far larger and far more important than anyone could have imagined as they shouted:

> "Hosanna!"
> "Blessed is he who comes in the name of the Lord!"
> "Blessed is the coming kingdom of our father David!"
> "Hosanna in the highest heaven!"
>
> MARK 11:9-10, NIV

I tend to make the same mistake those early followers made on Palm Sunday: I assume God is far smaller and more finite than he actually is.

I expect him to think about the world, about people around me, about my loved ones from my temporary, earthly, far-too-narrow perspective. When I assume God shares my temporary, earthly perspective, I am not aligned with his will, and I miss what he is doing.

God is sovereign, and he moves with eternity in mind. Our misaligned perspectives mean we cannot understand the fullness of what God is doing: "Now we see things imperfectly, like puzzling reflections in a mirror, but then we will see everything with perfect clarity. All that I know now is partial and incomplete, but then I will know everything completely, just as God now knows me completely" (1 Corinthians 13:12).

What does that mean for us, practically speaking? It means we walk by faith, not by sight (see 2 Corinthians 5:7). We are mindful that what we see with our eyes is temporary, that the eternal (the most important part) is not seen, and that we must embrace it by faith (see 2 Corinthians 4:18). We are people of faith with hope in the things that we cannot yet see, trusting in God for their fulfillment (see Hebrews 11:1).

This week we embrace relentless hope as people who stand on the cusp of Holy Week, reflecting on the redemptively hard events of those days, but also as people who await the return of our Savior. We are filled with hope for the future, resting in the assurance of God's sovereignty, his love, and his promises.

This Week's Fasting Focus

For our final weekly fast, we will guard against negative thoughts and words—toward ourselves and others. We will be people who speak life and encouragement over ourselves and those around us. We will be people who focus our faith on the eternal rather than the temporary. We will be people who bring the relentless hope found in Jesus into every room, every conversation, every situation.

What does this look like? It might mean we interrupt negative self-talk with Scripture we've selected beforehand. It might mean that we politely excuse ourselves from conversations when they take a negative turn about someone not in the room. It might mean we deflect invitations to gossip by shifting the conversation back toward people in the conversation, asking about their children, a recent trip, or something else they'd enjoy speaking about. Let us be people of hope who embrace an eternal perspective and take that hope into the world with us.

Heavenly Father, we acknowledge your goodness, your sovereignty, your eternal plan this Palm Sunday. Walk closely alongside us as we enter Holy Week. Do your work within us as we follow Jesus' footsteps to the cross and into his resurrection. Amen.

DAY 41

Equal Access

Jesus entered the Temple and began to drive out all the people buying and selling animals for sacrifice. He knocked over the tables of the money changers and the chairs of those selling doves. He said to them, "The Scriptures declare, 'My Temple will be called a house of prayer,' but you have turned it into a den of thieves!"

MATTHEW 21:12-13

"DOES ANYONE NEED A RIDE TO TRYOUTS?" I (Kendra) asked my son one fall day at suppertime.

"I'm not sure, but I can ask," he responded as he took a bite of spaghetti. "I'm sure there'll be a few guys."

"Okay, well, maybe put it on your group chat that your parents can bring anyone who needs a ride."

Abe smiled. "Yes, Mom."

"I just don't want anyone to get missed," I said.

My husband, Kyle, chuckled. "Don't worry, Kendra. I'll check as well."

Being a part of the soccer community in our hometown has been an enormous blessing to us—not the least of which is seeing the diverse group of young men and families who all come together over their love of the game. But along with that, we've had to be careful that no one is missed or overlooked. Factors we can easily take for granted, like transportation, flexible schedules, or two-parent homes, can be barriers or limitations to what other families can do or afford.

Being sensitive to everyone's circumstances and making sure their needs are met has become an important part of being in the community. It doesn't always go perfectly, and sometimes needs are missed. It's definitely been a learning experience, but one I'll humbly accept if it means we can see these young men come together on the field, finding they each have a spot, a place, with no one left out.

As I seek to grow in this area, Jesus provides the perfect example. On this Monday of Holy Week, we see that he was upset. Matthew tells us that "Jesus entered the Temple and began to drive out all the people buying and selling animals for sacrifice. He knocked over the tables of the money changers and the chairs of those selling doves. He said to them, 'The Scriptures declare, "My Temple will be called a house of prayer," but you have turned it into a den of thieves!'" (Matthew 21:12-13).

Why was he so mad? Because the people who were selling animals often charged exorbitant fees, putting undue pressure on travelers who wanted to offer sacrifices to God but couldn't afford it. The sellers were getting wealthy off the backs of the poor.

And in doing so, they left those people outside the realm of communing with God and worshiping in the ways that were expected at the time. A select group of people were leaving others out. If there's anything that makes Jesus angry, it's when humans oppress, weigh down, or abuse other human beings, who are also created in his image.

But the actions of those corrupt merchants didn't stop Jesus from his mission. He continued to go to the people who needed him the most. The following verses tell us,

> The blind and the lame came to him in the Temple, and he healed them. The leading priests and the teachers of religious law saw these wonderful miracles and heard even the children in the Temple shouting, "Praise God for the Son of David."
>
> But the leaders were indignant. They asked Jesus, "Do you hear what these children are saying?"
>
> "Yes," Jesus replied. "Haven't you ever read the Scriptures? For they say, 'You have taught children and infants to give you praise.'"
>
> MATTHEW 21:14-16

Jesus starts by driving out those who would take advantage of others. Then he notices and interacts with the most vulnerable among the remaining worshipers, healing them of their diseases and valuing the praises of the children—all things the religious leaders despised.

I often wonder if this was because the acclaim Jesus received threatened the leaders' power and privilege, their comfort and customs. They were accustomed to their station in life. They liked their position in society. Sometimes, that's harder to let go of than money or belongings. These were idols the leaders held closer and loved more than those around them.

Jesus' words were a strong admonishment for the people of his day, but they are also a warning to us reading the passage now. If we're honest, we can struggle with many of the same temptations they did. Money, power, position, and prestige still matter today, just as they did then. If we aren't careful, they can become idols in our lives too.

It's important to remember that the good news of Jesus is for us. But it is also for anyone else who will heed it. No one gets left out. Jesus breaks down barriers and invites everyone to come. He evens the playing field. No more in or out. He offers everyone a place.

Our challenge today is to ask ourselves, Do we do as Jesus does? Do we invite others in, or do we intentionally or even unintentionally keep them at a distance? Do we see others as Jesus sees them? Do we have an eternal perspective clearly in mind, one that offers hope to those around us?

We know that Jesus will strongly correct anyone who is not careful to love others the way he loves them. This doesn't mean that we have to feel guilty about the things we have, the place we live, or the position we hold in life. It does mean that we need to remain mindful of and sensitive to the needs of others. It means that we *notice*, just as Jesus did. We do not turn away from the most vulnerable. We offer to do something, to help, whenever we can.

Lord, thank you for breaking down the barriers that would hinder anyone from coming to you. Thank you that you care not only about our spiritual needs but about our physical and emotional needs as well. You meet us where we are, and we are grateful for that. Give us eyes to see all that you have given to us that we so easily take for granted. May we see all the ways that you've invited us in when others might not have. Help us to do the same for those around us. Give us an eternal perspective and help us see others through your eyes. Help us to look for ways to break down barriers and bring hope to others. We love you. Thank you for loving us. Amen.

For Reflection:

What barriers do we put up (intentionally or unintentionally) for those who desire to seek God? How can we ensure that everyone has access to Jesus and the hope he offers?

Sacred Rhythms:

Watch for opportunities to help remove barriers and bring hope to those around you, whether at school, work, or in your community. If appropriate, offer assistance.

Jesus breaks down barriers and invites everyone to come. No more in or out. He offers everyone a place.

DAY 42

Our Living Hope

Praise be to the God and Father of our Lord Jesus Christ! In his great mercy he has given us new birth into a living hope through the resurrection of Jesus Christ from the dead.

1 PETER 1:3, NIV

YEARS AGO, WHEN I (KRISTIN) WORKED for a newspaper, it was my job to read the paper from cover to cover to edit the copy and ensure that nothing had been overlooked. While the contents sometimes included inspiring and happy stories, they also contained reports of crime, loss, and deep pain. The total weight of those painful stories became so burdensome that, for a time, I had to change my leisure reading.

Instead of the romances and thrillers I usually favored, I began to read children's books. For several months, I rediscovered Roald Dahl's BFG (Big Friendly Giant), Laura Ingalls Wilder's pioneer days, the March sisters of Louisa May Alcott's *Little Women*, and the many Nancy Drew mystery books I'd once loved.

What I was looking for was a happy ending. I wanted wrongs to be righted and characters to be loved. I wanted resolutions, homecomings, and happiness. While the drama of real life promised only murky, often unsatisfying endings, children's books delivered the one thing I truly needed to be reminded of: hope. The hope of feeling purposeful, knowing who you are, and discovering who you could become. The hope that, even though bad things may happen, they'd turn out okay in the end.

Of course, life is more complex and nuanced than the stories in books. If we think what happens at the end is the only thing that matters, we miss the full scope of life. We miss the hope.

During Holy Week, that feels especially true. If the disciples had anticipated the agony of Friday, would they have so readily celebrated Jesus' triumphant entrance into Jerusalem the preceding Sunday? Did Friday's "bad ending" negate the good that came earlier?

Last year, I spent time rereading a journal I'd kept during my final year of college and the following year. Interspersed with discussions of work, my busy schedule, and what kind of car to lease were updates on my sister. Katrina had been sick with cancer off and on since I was sixteen, but by the time I wrote the journal, she'd gotten much worse. She experienced fractured bones, debilitating pain, and increasingly frequent hospital stays. By the end of my journal, tragically, she'd passed away at age twenty-eight. I was devastated.

If I were to hear my sister's story as a book synopsis, I might be tempted to pass it by. *No happy ending there*, I'd think. *How incredibly sad.*

And that is true. The loss of my sister was painful and premature. But if that were the only way I measured the sum of my sister's life—if all that mattered was whether or not her time on earth ended happily—oh, how much I would miss. The truth is that my sister's death didn't negate all the good things that happened in her life. Death cannot erase the sum of our lives. God's goodness remains.

Wondrously, that journal also reminded me of the glimpses of God's goodness my family witnessed over the years: the friends who dropped off meals or watched her kids, the woman who offered to clean her home, the nurse who privately told Katrina that she'd been praying for her for five years, the church members who rallied around her, and the hundreds of people who received her email updates and prayed diligently for her health and healing—many of whom she'd never even met. And those are just the stories I can recall.

All along, we prayed for a miracle: that God would heal Katrina of her cancer. He did, just not here on earth. So what does that mean for us? What does our faith mean if the miracle we pray for doesn't arrive?

Scripture talks a lot about running the race of faith and continuing that journey of faithfulness to the end. A passage in Romans reminds us that problems and trials are a reason to rejoice. They help us develop endurance and strengthen our character, and they lead to our "confident hope of salvation" (Romans 5:3-4). The next verse continues: "And this hope will not lead to disappointment. For we know how dearly God loves us, because he has given us the Holy Spirit to fill our hearts with his love" (verse 5).

The confident hope that we have in Jesus won't lead to disappointment. The Amplified Bible paraphrases verse 5 this way: "Such hope never disappoints or deludes or shames us" (AMPC). This is what 1 Peter 1:3 refers to as our "living hope" (NIV). The world is good at using our shame over what we perceive as failures to control or manipulate us. But God's love—and the hope it gives us of the world to come—overcomes that shame. The knowledge of eternity and our recognition that this world is not the end gives us hope to cling to and the freedom to move forward. Our trials beget our testimony of God's faithfulness when we recognize that this life isn't the end, even if our prayers aren't answered the way we think they should be. Either way, God is still good.

After all, during Holy Week, Friday wasn't really the end. By Sunday, Jesus would rise from the dead and then ascend to heaven, where we'll one day join him. The same is true for my sister—her earthly end simply marked the beginning of an eternity with Jesus. What an incredible ending! That is surely a reason to hold on to the living hope of salvation.

Jesus, thank you that no matter the highs and lows of our stories, we can take comfort in the living hope we have in you. On hard days, remind us of how you have demonstrated your faithfulness to us and others. When we are tempted to swallow the shame of parts of our stories, help us to remember that there's so much more to come. With you, we always have the hope of more. Thank you, Lord. Amen.

For Reflection:

How has the idea of the "living hope" we have in Jesus impacted your story? In what ways has experiencing difficulties in life led to greater faith in Jesus?

Sacred Rhythms:

Write the word hope *at the top of a blank page. Underneath it, jot down instances of God's faithfulness in past circumstances to remind yourself to have hope for hard days. Post it somewhere that you'll see it.*

This life isn't the end, even if our prayers aren't answered the way we think they should be. Either way, God is still good.

DAY 43

Jesus Is Our Hope

May our Lord Jesus Christ himself and God our Father, who loved us and by his grace gave us eternal comfort and a wonderful hope, comfort you and strengthen you in every good thing you do and say..

2 THESSALONIANS 2:16-17

AS THE YOUNGEST OF THREE GIRLS, I (Kristin) developed the habit early on of watching James Bond movies with my dad. He would always fast-forward through the parts that were too salacious or violent for a kid. By the time I was in high school, I relished seeing Sean Connery cruise down the road in a spectacular Aston Martin DB5 or the supervillain Ernst Stavro Blofeld pet his meowing white cat.

And, of course, I loved how James Bond always ended the movie victorious; good always defeated evil.

Despite my love of both spy movies and the Bible, I had never heard of "Spy Wednesday" until I was an adult. The idea behind this day is sobering: It was the fateful day when Judas approached the chief priests to ask for money to betray Jesus (although he wouldn't do so until the next day). At first glance, it would be easy to dismiss Judas as just one more villain, à la Ernst Stavro Blofeld. But a deeper look at Judas reveals that he was all too human, messy and flawed like the rest of us.

Judas was, at one point, sincere in his faith. He left his former life behind to follow Jesus and witnessed everything that Jesus did during their three years together, including his many miracles. Living side by side with the Savior, he was no mere acquaintance. He would have known Jesus' favorite meal, whether or not he snored or slept lightly, and when he was glad or weary. He would have witnessed and participated in the great work that Jesus did and the good news he shared.

So how does someone go from pouring their heart into the ministry of Jesus to becoming disenchanted and turning their back on it? No matter how sincere Judas was in the beginning, he became double-minded. John says he was a thief who stole from the disciples' collective money (see John 12:6). Like many sins, this thievery probably started small. Perhaps he stole a few coins or stashed them away for later. Maybe, over time, he took more, until his conscience no longer nagged at him. Perhaps he thought he deserved a more significant share or regretted the life he'd given up.

However it began, sin gave Satan a foothold into Judas's life. The ultimate reason for Judas's betrayal remains a mystery that the Gospels disagree on—Matthew's description signals that he was greedy, while Luke and John say that Satan entered him (see Matthew 26:14-16; Luke 22:3; John 13:27). Matthew says he was filled with remorse, threw the silver pieces in the Temple, and hanged himself (see Matthew 27:3-5). But in Acts, Peter says that Judas bought a field with the money, then fell headfirst and died (see Acts 1:18). Either way, it's a tragic conclusion to what could have been a beautiful story of redemption.

Whether he was a villain or a victim of larger circumstances, it remains difficult to comprehend how he could have betrayed Jesus. After all, Judas had listened to the best teacher and experienced the most compelling evidence of all—actual miracles!—yet he walked away. His experience proves that the external trappings of religion can never change the human heart. Judas ate, slept, and breathed next to the other disciples, but he still chose himself over the mission. His story is a crucial reminder that we must always guard our hearts lest we drift away.

The events of Holy Week also remind us of how frail and weak we can sometimes be. We are always only one small choice away from going down the wrong path. We feel compassion for Peter when he denies Jesus, and we understand why Thomas would doubt his return. Yet, Judas often receives our disdain for his actions. On Spy Wednesday, Judas's story is not the one that offers hope.

Our hope is found—as it always is—in Jesus. Jesus didn't loathe Judas, as we are tempted to do—he loved him. Even though Jesus must have known that Judas had been stealing from their coffers, he still invited him to walk alongside them from town to town, serving others and preaching the good news. Even though Jesus knew Judas would betray him, he continued to care for him. He washed his feet. He served him at the last supper. He didn't tell him not to betray him. Yes, it's Jesus who remains faithful to Judas, even knowing what he was going to do.

He does the same for you and me. He offers the same love and care, even knowing our weaknesses, our secret sins, and our regrets. Jesus is our hope, and even when we make mistakes, we can take comfort in knowing that God's plans aren't derailed by human error or failure. As Proverbs

19:21 reminds us, "You can make many plans, but the Lord's purpose will prevail."

How often have you or I done something and later regretted it? Though we may need to face consequences for our actions or ask forgiveness of those we've hurt, Jesus is willing to forgive us. His invitation remains open even when our intentions aren't good or our hearts are far from him. He is always ready, waiting, and willing to forgive. In him, we have a confident hope through the power of the Holy Spirit. We can find comfort in knowing that this hope will never disappoint.

Lord, thank you that your purposes prevail no matter what. Help us to recognize that we can always turn away from bad decisions or poor choices and ask you for help instead. It's never too late. Thank you for the comfort of knowing that no matter what happens in our lives, we can place our trust in you. In you, we have hope—now and forever. Your purposes remain firm. Amen.

For Reflection:

Do you see Judas as a villain, a victim, or simply a flawed human? How does knowing that Jesus always waits for us to turn from sins inspire hope?

Sacred Rhythms:

Spend time praying that you will be single-minded in pursuing Jesus, no matter the cost.

Jesus offers love and care for us, even knowing our weaknesses, our secret sins, and our regrets. Jesus is our hope, even when we make mistakes.

DAY 44

A Command to Love and Unity

I pray that they will all be one, just as you and I are one—as you are in me, Father, and I am in you. And may they be in us so that the world will believe you sent me.

JOHN 17:21

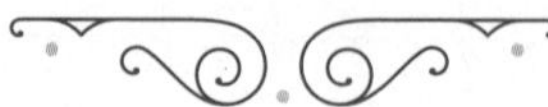

TODAY IS PERHAPS THE HARDEST DAY of Holy Week—at least for me (Julie)—because we witness Jesus' intentional choices, one after the other, that he knew would draw him ever closer to suffering and his ultimate crucifixion on Friday.

Jesus included Judas in the last supper, washing his betrayer's feet before sending him off, knowing exactly what he was leaving to do (see John 13:1-28).

Jesus retired with his remaining disciples to the garden of Gethsemane, where he prayed so fervently that he sweat drops of blood over what lay ahead and over those he loved, including both his contemporaries and those of us who were still to come (see Luke 22:44; John 17:1-26).

Jesus healed the ear of a Roman soldier (severed by Peter) even as he submitted to being arrested on false charges brought by the religious authorities (see Luke 22:49-51).

Jesus willingly submitted to a secret nighttime trial and horrendous physical abuse before the dawn of Friday and his journey to the crucifixion (see John 18:28–19:16).

Each decision, each step forward, testifies to Jesus' great love for us, unconditional and sacrificial. It's in these last hours that a clear theme and command for his disciples and for future believers—you and me—is set forth. In fact, that's why today is called Maundy Thursday in some traditions. The word *maundy* comes from the Latin *mandatum*, which translates to "command."

Jesus' sacrificial death as the final atonement for our sins is the new covenant, the new promise. And as Jesus prepared to make this sacrifice, his final instruction to believers of his day as well as to future believers (us) was one of unity and intentional love for one another.

We see this call to loving, mutual service and unity throughout Jesus' earthly ministry, but he doubles down on this command during his last hours.

Before eating what has become known as the last supper, Jesus modeled his expectations for how we are to treat one another by washing his disciples' feet, including Judas's:

> After washing their feet, he put on his robe again and sat down and asked, "Do you understand what I was doing? You call me 'Teacher' and 'Lord,' and you are right, because that's what I am. And since I, your Lord and Teacher, have washed your feet, you ought to wash each other's feet. I have given you an example

> to follow. Do as I have done to you. I tell you the truth, slaves are not greater than their master. Nor is the messenger more important than the one who sends the message."
>
> JOHN 13:12-16

In that culture, it was customary for a household servant to wash guests' feet before a meal. With the primary footwear being sandals, feet were dusty and dirty. Tables were situated low to the ground, and no one wanted dusty feet near their food. In taking on the job of the household servant, Jesus modeled servant leadership and humility by washing feet before commanding the disciples to do the same for one another. Our earthly hierarchies based upon wealth, influence, and power are worthless in God's eyes. We are called to both humility and loving community with one another (see Matthew 5:38-40; 20:16; Galatians 5:13; James 4:10).

But it is Jesus' prayer in the garden of Gethsemane that brings me to tears, year after year. He prays for protection, for joy, and for the teaching he has imparted to his followers. But then he turns his attention to include not only his current followers in his prayer, but also every future believer, including you and me:

> I am praying not only for these disciples but also for all who will ever believe in me through their message. I pray that they will all be one, just as you and I are one—as you are in me, Father, and I am in you. And may they be in us so that the world will believe you sent me.
>
> I have given them the glory you gave me, so they may be one as we are one. I am in them and you are in me. *May they*

> *experience such perfect unity that the world will know that you sent me and that you love them as much as you love me.* Father, I want these whom you have given me to be with me where I am. Then they can see all the glory you gave me because you loved me even before the world began!
>
> JOHN 17:20-24, EMPHASIS ADDED

His prayer was that we would be unified both with God and in community with one another. And he indicates that our unity would *convince the world* of two things: (1) that God sent Jesus to deliver us from sin, and (2) that God loves each of us as much as he loves Jesus. If we—as followers of Jesus—could figure out how to live in loving, unified community with one another, we would convince the world of the truth.

It was during a long-ago Holy Week that I first encountered this revelation in my reread of John 17. I paused, surprised and excited by the firmness of this promise. Why hadn't I heard this before? Why weren't we talking about this? Where were the books on this teaching?[1] How could a promise like this be skipped over by everyone I'd listened to and learned from up to that point?

And then I opened a newspaper app and wept. An article described how a charismatic church leader had abused his power and hurt people in his congregation. Next to that headline was one in which a political leader was wielding out-of-context Scripture to gain power and influence. Those articles simply reflected on a bigger stage the un-Christlike behavior that goes on in smaller faith communities or between church communities.

Rather than lose hope in the face of such headlines, I use those moments to double down on living out Jesus' command toward unity. I recommit to living a life that reveals the good news, so that my actions support what my tongue professes. I desperately want to be part of the solution, part of the invitation into the freedom of life in Christ. I want to be a unifier, a person of eternal perspective and hope who rallies others into a healthy faith community rather than someone who sows discord and division.

That requires thoughtful intentionality and—often—not demanding my preference or my way in my faith communities. I'm not a doormat, but I consider where people are on their own faith journey and how I can encourage progress and growth for the entire community, sometimes to my own inconvenience or contrary to my preference. This is not easy, and it will almost certainly look different for you than it does for me. In a world that loves chaos, it's a challenge to live as a unifier.

Please believe me when I say that God uses imperfect people to accomplish his will. There is grace for mistakes and for learning to do better. (Redemptive forgiveness is what Holy Week is all about.) As we commit to the work of unity, even imperfectly, we grow closer to the promise that the world will be convinced that Jesus was sent to redeem us simply by how well we love one another. And that, my friends, is powerful.

One quick note: Unity is not uniformity. We are told that every language and culture will be represented in heaven (see Revelation 7:9). Unity is not a situation in which everyone must adapt to your preferred ways or the preferred ways of your denominational culture. Part of living in unity among other believers is making space for people who have a different religious tradition within Christianity. While we must agree upon a few core teachings, how we go about loving God and loving one another will look different (see 1 Corinthians 12:12-14).

If this stings, know that it is convicting for me too. Living in loving unity with fellow followers of Jesus can be intensely challenging. But the struggle to create and maintain healthy faith communities is worth the effort. We must show the world the transformational love of Jesus through our actions *and* our words. The world will not (and obviously does not) believe our declarations without actions to back them up.

Heavenly Father, help us be people who are unifiers within the family of Christ. Give us grace for ourselves and others when we fall short, but keep us moving forward as people who embody the fruits of the Spirit: love, joy, peace, patience, kindness, goodness, faithfulness, gentleness, and self-control (see Galatians 5:22-23). May our actions reflect our faith. Amen.

For Reflection:

Consider ways you could encourage unity within your own faith community or circle of fellow believers.

Sacred Rhythms:

Pick one idea from your reflection and do it well.

Living in loving unity can be intensely challenging. But the struggle to create and maintain healthy faith communities is worth the effort.

DAY 45

Where Is Death's Sting?

At noon, darkness fell across the whole land until three o'clock. Then at three o'clock Jesus called out with a loud voice, "Eloi, Eloi, lema sabachthani?" which means "My God, my God, why have you abandoned me?". . . Then Jesus uttered another loud cry and breathed his last. And the curtain in the sanctuary of the Temple was torn in two, from top to bottom.

MARK 15:33-34, 37-38

I WALKED SLOWLY to the front of the sanctuary. My hands shook as I (Kendra) opened my small notebook. Looking out over the grieving crowd, I felt my throat tighten with emotion. I wanted to speak in memory of my uncle; my aunt had made it clear she'd like me to, but I was scared. And so, so sad.

I still had not fully grasped that my uncle was gone, taken so suddenly by a heart attack that he most likely didn't even realize was happening. In some ways, we were comforted by this thought. At least we don't believe he suffered. Even so, it was hard to think that he was gone.

I can still hear my uncle's belly laugh and his booming voice that would rise and fall as he told stories about our family. He had a memory that could conjure up tales from a week ago or from years prior. He loved his family. And his farm—the land on which he'd raised kids and animals alike. He was a part of everything I remember, woven deep into the fabric of my childhood.

He was so full of life that it was hard to believe he was gone.

I took in a deep breath as I looked down at my notebook. The frayed edges of the pages where I'd scribbled notes seemed reminiscent of my life, which somehow felt frayed as well.

My aunt gave me a small smile from the front row as I told stories about my uncle. Little things he'd done. Songs he'd made up and sung without any inhibition. Ways he'd shown love over the years.

"Jimmy loved Jesus," I said. "He wasn't a man who shared a lot about what he believed. But he lived a simple faith, one filled with love for God and others around him."

My throat constricted as I paused. Even now, I hate the way I'll sometimes be overcome with emotion, unable to convey everything I want to say.

". . . And I know that we'll see him again. Death does not have the final say," I barely whispered. "First Corinthians 15:54-57 says, 'Then, when our dying bodies have been transformed into bodies that will never die, this Scripture will be fulfilled: "Death is swallowed up in victory. O death, where is your victory? O death, where is your sting?" For sin is the sting that results in death, and the law gives sin its power. But thank God! He gives us victory over sin and death through our Lord Jesus Christ.'"

I finished with more boldness than I'd started. My cousin nodded, I smiled back as I walked down the steps to sit with the rest of our family, and the service continued.

At the very core of my being, I knew that what I had shared was true. Death has no lasting sting because it has been swallowed up in victory. And that victory came on Calvary when Jesus chose to give himself for us. Jesus died so that we might know death is not the final outcome. There is always life after death. He died so that we might know how to live, and to remind us to follow him in laying down our lives for others.

He came to show us who the Father had always been and how much he loves us. The curtain that separated man from God was torn from top to bottom when Jesus died. Some scholars believe the construction of this sentence indicates that God was the one who tore the veil to open the way to himself.

On this day, we remember and grieve all those who have died before us, the loved ones we ache to see again. It's okay to feel that way. We do suffer when death occurs. We grieve. Allowing ourselves to do so is right and needed.

Yet we hold this day with hope. Grief and expectation mix together because we know death is not the end of the story. It wasn't the end for Jesus. It's not the end for our loved ones. And it won't be the end for us.

Sit in all that is somber today, but remember the words of Isaiah, knowing they have come true, just as God promised.

There he will remove the cloud of gloom,
    the shadow of death that hangs over the earth.
He will swallow up death forever!
    The Sovereign Lord will wipe away all tears.

ISAIAH 25:7-8

Lord Jesus, thank you for this day. On this Good Friday, we remember your suffering and your death on the cross. For us. As we reflect on your sacrifice, show us a way through death into life. May we take the time to sit with the sorrow of the cross. May we never forget your sacrificial love, given to us and for us. We sit in the grief of this day with hopeful expectation of what is to come. You are not finished, and death does not have the final say. May we be reminded of this as we grieve loved ones no longer with us on earth. Victory is on the way. Our hope is secure. We love you. Thank you for loving us. Amen.

For Reflection:

How can remembering what Jesus did for us on this day help us deal with our grief over those we've lost?

Sacred Rhythms:

Reread Isaiah 25:7-8 and reflect on the promise we have of seeing our loved ones again. Allow yourself to grieve while remembering all that God has promised.

Grief and expectation mix together because we know death is not the end of the story. It wasn't the end for Jesus. It's not the end for our loved ones. And it won't be the end for us.

DAY 46

We Are Not Abandoned

Be sure of this: I am with you always, even to the end of the age.

MATTHEW 28:20

"LORD, I FEEL ALONE IN THIS. Where are you?!"

Shoulders hunched in surprise at the vehemence of that outburst, a decade-younger version of me (Julie) scanned the skies from her spot in the grocery store parking lot. One does not shout angrily at Jesus from the driver's seat of her baby-blue minivan without immediately pondering the possibility of being thunderbolted.

Seeing no lightning strike from heaven and recognizing the deep well of emotion masquerading as anger, I burst into tears over something I have since forgotten. While I can't recall the why, I vividly remember the feeling: overwhelmed and alone, abandoned by Jesus in that moment.

Was I abandoned? Of course not, and it didn't take long for my rational mind to catch up with my runaway emotions. But I've thought of this moment every year since during the pause between Jesus' death on Friday afternoon and his resurrection on Sunday.

Because we know the ending to the story (an empty tomb and a risen king on Easter), we can tend to skip over the turmoil and angst roiling below the quietness of that first Holy Saturday. How must those following Jesus have felt as the sun set Friday night, ushering in the Sabbath? I imagine they experienced a bewildered, desperate grief, with expectations and hope shattered and replaced by immense fear and chaos.

But here's the thing: Just because it seemed quiet then does not mean Jesus was not at work on behalf of all humanity. And just because Jesus seems quiet in our struggles now does not mean he is not at work for us. We are never abandoned. We are never left alone. On this, Scripture is clear in today's verse as well as in Romans 8:38-39:

> I am convinced that nothing can ever separate us from God's love. Neither death nor life, neither angels nor demons, neither our fears for today nor our worries about tomorrow—not even the powers of hell can separate us from God's love. No power in the sky above or in the earth below—indeed, nothing in all creation will ever be able to separate us from the love of God that is revealed in Christ Jesus our Lord.

What his followers saw as failure and abandonment on that quiet Saturday was Jesus seizing the keys to Hades and once and for all reclaiming victory over death on our behalf. That silent stretch of time between the horrors of Friday and the celebration of Sunday is among the most important hours in human history. But to those who had been following

Jesus, it felt like silence. Like abandonment. Like abject failure. Like all had been lost.

Friend, no matter the hard circumstance you are facing, you do not walk in it alone. Even when God feels distant, he is not. You are not abandoned. Jesus is with you, even to the end of the age.

As we end the last of these weeks together, be sure to continue to the weekly reflection on the following page as part of today's reading. And don't miss Resurrection Sunday!

Just because Jesus seems quiet in our struggles now does not mean he is not at work for us. We are never abandoned. We are never left alone.

For Further Reflection

1. What stood out to you this week about maintaining an eternal perspective and embracing a relentless hope? What surprised or inspired you? What tested or challenged you?

2. What insights did you gain through this week's fast from negative thoughts and words? Were you able to instead speak life and encouragement over yourself and others?

3. Where do you struggle to keep an eternal perspective and embrace hope, and where can you work to improve?

Lord, thank you that this silent Saturday serves as a tangible, yearly reminder that what might feel like abandonment does not mean you are not at work behind the scenes. Thank you for the world-changing work you accomplished on this quiet day. Help us to remember that you never forsake us nor abandon us. Amen.

EASTER WEEK

JOY

Resurrection Sunday

DAY 47

He Is Risen!

Early on Sunday morning, as the new day was dawning, Mary Magdalene and the other Mary went out to visit the tomb. Suddenly there was a great earthquake! For an angel of the Lord came down from heaven, rolled aside the stone, and sat on it. His face shone like lightning, and his clothing was as white as snow. The guards shook with fear when they saw him, and they fell into a dead faint. Then the angel spoke to the women. "Don't be afraid!" he said. "I know you are looking for Jesus, who was crucified. He isn't here! He is risen from the dead, just as he said would happen."

MATTHEW 28:1-6

THE TWO MARYS MET BEFORE DAWN, when the shadows of night were just breaking. I (Kendra) often wonder if they wanted to avoid seeing people who were going out to start their day. Since the two women would have been easily recognizable, some may have whispered behind their backs, while others brazenly asked what happened. The women may have been trying to avoid such encounters.

I'm sure they were also grieving. A place of deep sorrow is not always one you want to share with others, especially when their motives aren't always loving or kind.

As the women walked the path toward the burial place of Jesus, something didn't look quite right. Maybe they thought it was just the shifting shadows as the day began. But then they saw clearly. I wonder what they noticed first—the stone rolled aside, or the angel sitting on top of it, as if he'd been waiting for them.

Either way, as they approached, they had no idea that in a single interaction—just a few words from the angel—their expectations and their very future would be changed in a moment. Because he was there with good news.

"Jesus is not here! He is risen! Just as he said it would happen."

Oh, what joy! It was too great to fathom.

We started this season of Lent in a garden, so it seems fitting to end in a garden. God's first interaction with humanity resulted in separation, pain, and sin. But this time, there would be forgiveness, unity, and joy.

We've come full circle, to a completion. God has pursued humanity again and again. It's not the end of the story, but a new beginning.

We opened with God's pursuit of us and a promise from Revelation 21:3: "I heard a loud voice from the throne saying, 'Look! God's dwelling place is now among the people, and he will dwell with them. They will be his people, and God himself will be with them and be their God'" (NIV).

It's a beautiful promise, but that's not all of it. Verses 4 and 5 go on to say, "'He will wipe every tear from their eyes. There will be no more death' or mourning or crying or pain, for the old order of things has passed away. He who was seated on the throne said, 'I am making everything new!'" (NIV).

Hallelujah! Our Savior has come! He is with us. He has defeated death and taken back the keys of the grave, and he is seated on the throne as King. We no longer have to fear death because he overcame it.

And he promises that someday there will be no more crying or pain. Every tear he will wipe from our eyes. How we long for the day when he makes all things new, and what great hope we have in him as we wait.

But we aren't called to simply wait for Jesus' return. He wants more for us and from us.

Before Jesus ascended to heaven forty days after his resurrection, he invited the first disciples to continue following him by going out to tell others the good news: God has come. He is our rescue, our hope, and our salvation.

> Jesus came and told his disciples, "I have been given all authority in heaven and on earth. Therefore, go and make disciples of all the nations, baptizing them in the name of the Father and the Son and the Holy Spirit. Teach these new disciples to obey all the commands I have given you. And be sure of this: I am with you always, even to the end of the age."
>
> MATTHEW 28:18-20

His pursuit of us continues today. He calls to us, inviting us in as family, into an intimate relationship with him. He desires to walk with us daily, and he reminds us that he is with us always. Safe and secure in his presence, we now go with him to others who desperately need to know of his love, forgiveness, and mercy, and to know that he will never stop pursuing them.

Now able to see clearly as his ambassadors, we have the privilege of following Jesus and modeling a life of love expressed in word and deed.

As we finish this Lenten journey, we hope that you will understand how much God has pursued you. Join us on a mission with him to pursue those who need to know that same truth. Unity with God and unity with others, the joining of heaven and earth—this is still at the very heart of who God is.

Will we say yes to his call today?

Lord, thank you for pursuing us from the very beginning. Thank you for coming to earth to show us who you are and for teaching us how to live as your followers. Thank you for dying, defeating death, and returning to life. We praise your name and celebrate with all of creation! We're humbled and honored that you now ask us to go out as your disciples and tell others the good news for all people: that you have come to seek and to save. That you love us with an everlasting love. May we forever be in awe of how wide, deep, and endless your love is, and may we have a fresh view today of your pursuit of us, of all humanity. May it offer us the courage to go out and love the world around us. Amen.

For Reflection:

What is your biggest takeaway from the past few weeks of walking through God's pursuit of you and all of humanity? What does it mean to go out with him in pursuit of others now?

Sacred Rhythms:

Write down practical ways you will live as Jesus' disciple by loving God and others in the coming days, months, and years.

Hallelujah! Our Savior has come! He has taken back the keys of the grave, and he is seated on the throne.

Appendix

Breath Prayers

WEEK 1: PURSUIT

Lord, I seek you. (2 Chronicles 15:2)

Inhale: God who pursues us,

Exhale: Draw me closer to you.

WEEK 2: LOVE

Help us to love you and those around us. (Matthew 22:35-40)

Inhale: God who is love,

Exhale: Help me be loving.

WEEK 3: FORGIVENESS

Forgive us our sins, as we forgive others. (Matthew 6:12)

Inhale: God who forgives freely,

Exhale: May I do the same.

WEEK 4: PEACE AND CONTENTMENT

The peace of Christ rules my heart. (Colossians 3:15)

Inhale: Prince of Peace,

Exhale: Reign in my heart.

WEEK 5: GENEROSITY

The Lord is my shepherd and gives me all I need. (Psalm 23:1)

Inhale: Shepherd of my soul,

Exhale: All I need is in you.

WEEK 6: FREEDOM

Where the Spirit of the Lord is, I have freedom. (2 Corinthians 3:17)

Inhale: Lord who is near,

Exhale: Break the chains that bind.

HOLY WEEK: HOPE

Lord, you are faithful; I hold fast to hope. (Hebrews 10:23)

Inhale: Faithful Father,

Exhale: My every hope is in you.

Fasting Ideas for Individuals

Why do we fast? Fasting enables us to be mindful of all the things we've received (and sometimes taken for granted), to sacrifice something (even if it's just our preferences), to remember God throughout our day, and to find ways to show love to others.

- Embrace your denomination's traditional fasting requirements.
- Give up your favorite drink for the day.
- Fast from one meal each day.
- Give up a certain amount of social media time and spend that time with God instead.
- Fast from a modern-day convenience (the stove, microwave, or dishwasher), and as you go throughout your day, pray for people who live without basic necessities we take for granted.
- Walk, bike, or ride the bus instead of driving your car.
- Fast from going out to eat for a time.
- Fast from makeup, perfume, or jewelry (choose one or all three).
- Exchange your current playlists for worship music or silence.
- If you have a reserved parking spot or other "special treatment," forgo that perk.
- Fast from a particular type of food (chocolate, caffeine, sugar, etc.).
- Rather than fasting, *add* a daily prayer walk around your neighborhood.
- Rather than fasting, *add* daily or weekly volunteer service to your Lenten journey.
- Rather than fasting, *add* a daily connection to extended family or friends, letting them know you are thinking of them and praying for them.
- Rather than fasting, *add* twenty minutes of silence to your daily routine, stilling yourself before God.

Fasting Ideas for Kids/Families

- Give up your favorite treat or drink for the day.
- Decrease your screen time each day by a certain amount (15 minutes/30 minutes/1 hour) and instead use that time for having family devotionals, playing a game together, going for a walk, or some other family activity.
- Instead of going out to eat, use the money to purchase a gift card to bless someone else this week.
- Spend some time writing thank-you cards to teachers, family members, or friends, and tell them something you appreciate about them.
- When walking through your neighborhood, write encouraging messages in chalk on the sidewalk.
- Rather than fasting, *add* a daily musical dance party with an upbeat worship song.
- Rather than fasting, *add* a daily conversation involving both thanking God for his provision and prayer for others.
- Rather than fasting, *add* a weekly Scripture memorization component to your family's Lenten journey.
- Rather than fasting, *add* a kindness challenge to your family's Lenten journey.
- Rather than fasting, *add* a weekly volunteering or service project.

Notes

DAY 3: CHASING SUNSETS

1. University of Exeter, "The Magic of Sunrise and Sunset: New Research Quantifies the 'Wow' Factor," SciTechDaily, March 18, 2023, https://scitechdaily.com/the-magic-of-sunrise-and-sunset-new-research-quantifies-the-wow-factor/.

DAY 8: BECAUSE HE FIRST LOVED US

1. Child Welfare Information Gateway, *Helping Your Adopted Children Maintain Important Relationships with Family* (US Department of Health and Human Services, Administration for Children and Families, Children's Bureau, 2019), https://cwig-prod-prod-drupal-s3fs-us-east-1.s3.amazonaws.com/public/documents/factsheets_families_maintainrelationships.pdf.

DAY 12: HEALED INSIDE AND OUT

1. Laura Yuen, "Her Story of Forgiveness Helped Others Heal—Now They're Helping Her Remember It," *Star Tribune*, May 11, 2023, https://www.startribune.com/mary-johnson-roy-dementia-homicide-forgiveness-from-death-to-life-oshea-israel/600274081/.

DAY 13: ONE-SIDED FORGIVENESS

1. Louise B. Miller, "What Causes Anger and How It Affects the Body," *Psychology Today*, July 16, 2020, https://www.psychologytoday.com/us/blog/the-mind-body-connection/202007/what-causes-anger-and-how-it-affects-the-body.

DAY 14: FORGIVING GOD

1. If you'd like to explore this topic further, I have found the following authors to be especially helpful: Greg Boyd; N. T. Wright; and Craig Groeschel, especially his book *Hope in the Dark*.

DAY 15: THE POWER OF AN APOLOGY

1. Dictionary.com, "repent," accessed April 4, 2024, https://www.dictionary.com/browse/repent.

DAY 16: THE STORIES WE TELL OURSELVES

1. Charity Ferreira, "8 Tips for Forgiving Someone Who Hurt You," *Stanford Magazine*, December 12, 2019, https://stanfordmag.org/contents/8-tips-for-forgiving-someone-who-hurt-you.

DAY 23: ALL THAT WE NEED

1. Misty Pratt, "The Science of Gratitude," Mindful, February 17, 2022, https://www.mindful.org/the-science-of-gratitude/.

DAY 33: FREEDOM IN CHRIST

1. Seyma Bayram, "Billions of People Lack Access to Clean Drinking Water, U.N. Report Finds," NPR, March 22, 2023, https://www.npr.org/2023/03/22/1165464857/billions-of-people-lack-access-to-clean-drinking-water-u-n-report-finds.
2. "Food," Global Issues, United Nations, accessed February 25, 2025, https://www.un.org/en/global-issues/food.

DAY 35: FREEDOM FROM WORRY

1. Michelle Pugle, "Can Stress Cause Death?," PsychCentral, June 30, 2022, https://psychcentral.com/stress/is-stress-the-number-one-killer.
2. Caitlin Mazur, "40+ Worrisome Workplace Stress Statistics [2023]: Facts, Causes, and Trends," Zippia, February 11, 2023, https://www.zippia.com/advice/workplace-stress-statistics/.

DAY 37: FREEDOM FROM SHAME

1. Brené Brown, *Daring Greatly: How the Courage to Be Vulnerable Transforms the Way We Live, Love, Parent, and Lead* (Penguin, 2012), 67–69.
2. *Baker's Evangelical Dictionary of Biblical Theology*, "Fellowship," by Peter Toon, Bible Study Tools, accessed February 2, 2025, https://www.biblestudytools.com/dictionary/fellowship/.
3. Brown, *Daring Greatly*, 74.

DAY 44: A COMMAND TO LOVE AND UNITY

1. Francis Chan has since written a book on this topic called *Until Unity.*

About the Authors

JULIE FISK left a fifteen-year legal career to become an author. Always passionate about words, she shifted her storytelling from courtrooms and boardrooms to telling stories of God's faithfulness, no matter the circumstance. Julie is a national speaker and coauthor of several books. Together with her cofounders of The Ruth Experience, Julie connects with an online community of women seeking and living out their faith. When she's not writing or speaking, Julie is a backyard farmer, a collector of coffee mugs, and an admitted bookworm.

Do it afraid. **KENDRA ROEHL** has sought to live out that advice as a social worker, foster parent, mother of five, and public speaker. She has a master's degree in social work and has naturally become a defender of those in need, serving others in hospice, low-income housing, and veterans' affairs programs. Kendra and her husband are well-known advocates for foster care, taking in more than twenty children in six years and adopting three of them. As a cofounder of The Ruth Experience, she continues to care for others as a frequent speaker and an author of several books.

A career in journalism set KRISTIN DEMERY up to one day publish her own stories of living this wild, precious life. She is now an author of several books and part of a trio of writers collectively known as The Ruth Experience. Kristin served as a newspaper and magazine editor, and her work has been featured in a variety of publications, including *USA Today*. She still works behind the scenes as an editor for others while writing her own series on kindness, friendship, and living with intention. An adventurer at heart, she loves checking items off the family bucket list with her husband and three daughters.

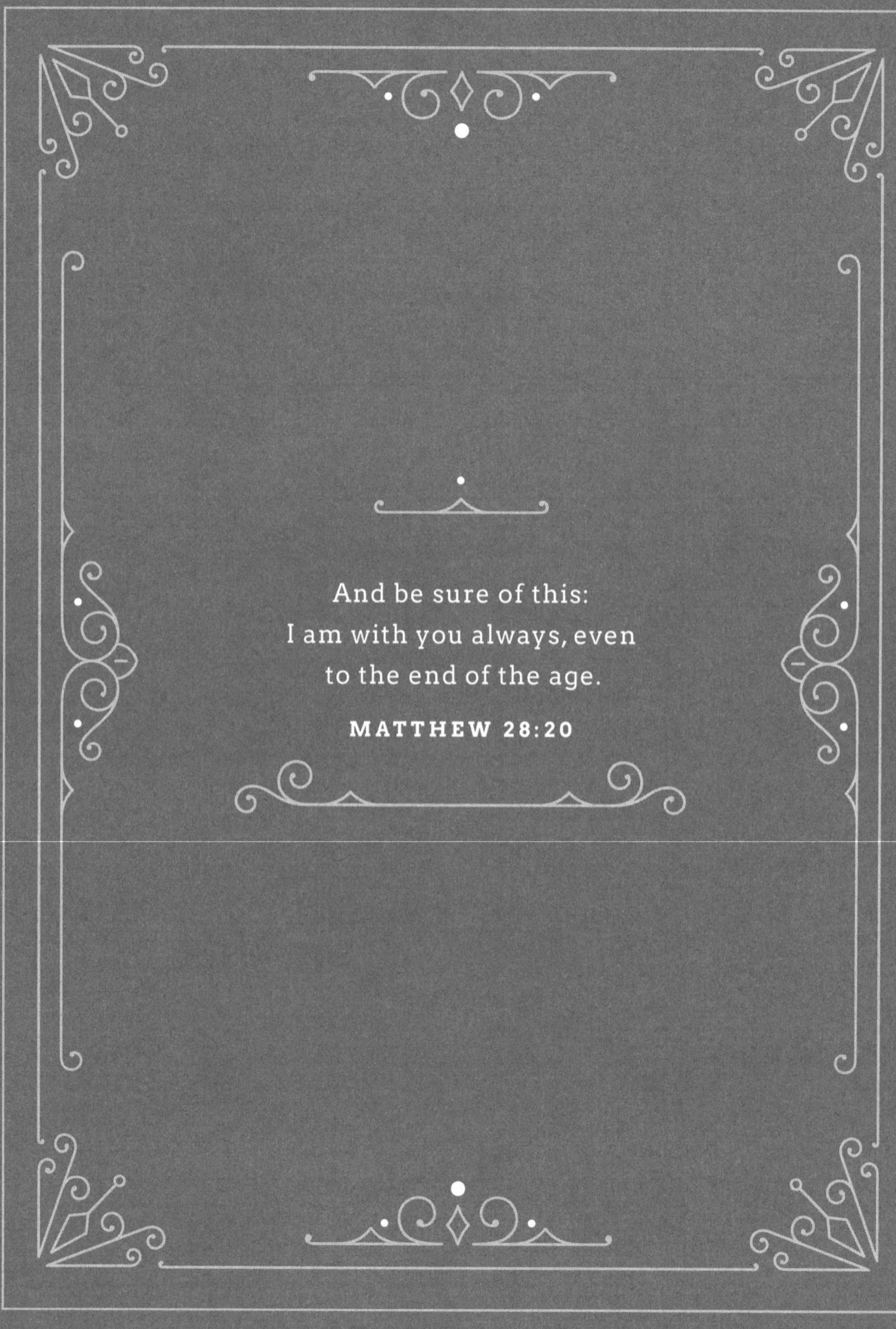

And be sure of this:
I am with you always, even
to the end of the age.

MATTHEW 28:20